THE HISTORY OF NATIONS

Japan

Other books in the History of Nations series:

Canada

China

England

Germany

India

Iraq

Italy

North Korea

Pakistan

Russia

Spain

THE HISTORY OF NATIONS

Japan

Clay Farris Naff, *Book Editor*

Daniel Leone, *President*
Bonnie Szumski, *Publisher*
Scott Barbour, *Managing Editor*

GREENHAVEN
PRESS®

THOMSON
GALE

San Diego • Detroit • New York • San Francisco • Cleveland
New Haven, Conn. • Waterville, Maine • London • Munich

For more information, contact
Greenhaven Press
27500 Drake Rd.
Farmington Hills, MI 48331-3535
Or you can visit our Internet site at http://www.gale.com

LIBRARY OF CONGRESS CATALOGING-IN-PUBLICATION DATA
Japan / Clay Farris Naff, book editor.
p. cm. — (History of nations)
Includes bibliographical references and index.
ISBN 0-7377-1857-9 (pbk. : alk. paper) — ISBN 0-7377-1856-0 (lib. : alk. paper)
1. Japan—History. I. Naff, Clay Farris. II. History of nations (Greenhaven Press)
DS835.J373 2004
952—dc21   2003048325

CONTENTS

Chapter 1: Ancient Japan

1. The Founding Myth
by the Kojiki

Mythology tells of the creation of Japan by the gods
and of an unbroken line of emperors descended from
the gods. This line of emperors is said to have begun
with Jimmu in 660 B.C.

2. Prehistory and the Jōmon Era
by Kenneth G. Henshall

The earliest culture in Japan dates from about 13,000
B.C. The name Jōmon refers to the people, their style
of pottery, and the era in which they lived.

Chapter 2: The Medieval Era

1. Feudal Lords Fight for Power
by Kenneth Scott Latourette

From the late twelfth to the late fifteenth centuries,
various warlords fought for control of Japan.

2. Europeans Reach Japan
by Ian Nish

In 1542, a group of shipwrecked Portuguese sailors
washed up on Japan's shores. They were soon followed by a missionary named Francis Xavier and Portuguese and Dutch traders.

3. Japan Closes Its Doors
by Kenneth G. Henshall

Ieyasu, founder of the Tokugawa dynasty, and his successors put a stop to the influence of foreigners by
banning Christianity, expelling foreigners, and sealing
off Japan from the world.

Chapter 6: Japan's Clouded Future

FOREWORD

I n 1841, the journalist Charles MacKay remarked, "In reading the history of nations, we find that, like individuals, they have their whims and peculiarities, their seasons of excitement and recklessness." At the time of MacKay's observation, many of the nations explored in the Greenhaven Press History of Nations series did not yet exist in their current form. Nonetheless, whether it is old or young, every nation is similar to an individual, with its own distinct characteristics and unique story.

The History of Nations series is dedicated to exploring these stories. Each anthology traces the development of one of the world's nations from its earliest days, when it was perhaps no more than a promise on a piece of paper or an idea in the mind of some revolutionary, through to its status in the world today. Topics discussed include the pivotal political events and power struggles that shaped the country as well as important social and cultural movements. Often, certain dramatic themes and events recur, such as the rise and fall of empires, the flowering and decay of cultures, or the heroism and treachery of leaders. As well, in the history of most countries war, oppression, revolution, and deep social change feature prominently. Nonetheless, the details of such events vary greatly, as does their impact on the nation concerned. For example, England's "Glorious Revolution" of 1688 was a peaceful transfer of power that set the stage for the emergence of democratic institutions in that nation. On the other hand, in China, the overthrow of dynastic rule in 1912 led to years of chaos, civil war, and the eventual emergence of a Communist regime that used violence as a tool to root out opposition and quell popular protest. Readers of the Greenhaven Press History of Nations series will learn about the common challenges nations face and the different paths they take in response to such crises. However a nation's story may have developed, the series strives to present a clear and unbiased view of the country at hand.

The structure of each volume in the series is designed to help students deepen their understanding of the events, movements, and persons that define nations. First, a thematic introduction provides critical background material and helps orient the reader. The chapters themselves are designed to provide an accessible and engaging approach to the study of the history of that nation involved and are arranged either thematically or chronologically, as appropriate. The selections include both primary documents, which convey something of the flavor of the time and place concerned, and secondary material, which includes the wisdom of hindsight and scholarship. Finally, each book closes with a detailed chronology, a comprehensive bibliography of suggestions for further research, and a thorough index.

The countries explored within the series are as old as China and as young as Canada, as distinct in character as Spain and India, as large as Russia, and as compact as Japan. Some are based on ethnic nationalism, the belief in an ethnic group as a distinct people sharing a common destiny, whereas others emphasize civic nationalism, in which what defines citizenship is not ethnicity but commitment to a shared constitution and its values. As human societies become increasingly globalized, knowledge of other nations and of the diversity of their cultures, characteristics, and histories becomes ever more important. This series responds to the challenge by furnishing students with a solid and engaging introduction to the history of the world's nations.

Japan: A History of Extremes

Japan is so fascinating in part because it often seems so bewildering. As the famed British diplomat and historian of Japan Sir George Sansom put it just after World War II, "Few countries have been more copiously described than Japan, and perhaps few have been less thoroughly understood." Home to one of the world's oldest civilizations and most advanced societies, Japan remains one of the most difficult nations for outsiders to grasp.

The Japanese people themselves have long believed their ways are incomprehensible to outsiders. Tokyo-born historian Edwin Reischauer considered that the first and greatest obstacle was the Japanese language itself. "Possessing a writing system more complex than any other," he wrote, "and a language with no close relatives, the Japanese probably face a bigger language barrier between themselves and the rest of the world than does any other major national group."

Many other difficulties face those who want to understand Japanese history, culture, and government. Although the country's four main islands lie close to the Asian mainland, the Japanese never became a seafaring people and chose for much of their history to remain in splendid isolation. At various times, scholars were sent abroad to study the ways of foreigners, but what they brought back was deliberately and carefully "Japanized." Living for centuries in cramped and often violent circumstances, the Japanese developed great skill in masking their feelings, disguising their meanings, and playing their roles.

Fortunately, since World War II a vast new effort has been made to engage the so-called Land of the Rising Sun. This anthology contains many knowledgeable essays that present a variety of perspectives on Japan's history and its people. Through the writings of Japanese men and women, visitors to the country, and historians who have studied the nation's long history, readers can begin to understand the events and traditions that make Japan unique.

A Nation of Contrasts

In almost every aspect, Japan presents contrasts, and in many instances the contrasts are acute. Throughout its history Japan has veered from one extreme to another. It has, at times, been the most warlike nation in Asia and, at others, the most pacifist. It was one of the last civilizations to acquire writing but the first to produce a novel. Japanese men have cultivated both extreme masculinity, embodied in the samurai warrior, and effeminacy, exemplified in the *onnagata* (men who play the roles of women in Japan's unique kabuki theater). Among women, femininity has been taken to such extremes that single women often speak in artificially high-pitched "little girl" voices, yet middle-aged women often put on a gruff, masculine persona.

Within the extremes lie many paradoxes. The foundations of Japan's culture are mostly borrowings from abroad, and yet they support one of the most distinctive societies in the world. Japan's writing system was adapted from Chinese, but the differences between the two languages make it impossible for Chinese and Japanese to converse, or even read each other's language to any great extent. One of Japan's two main religions, Buddhism, came from India through China, whereas the other, Shinto, emerged from ancient Japanese nature worship. So which do most Japanese follow? Both!

Rugged and Beautiful Geography

A tendency toward the extreme seems to be sown into the very land. Japan's four main islands and numerous minor ones form a jagged crescent off the eastern shore of Asia. Altogether, the country is about the size of California. However, it displays a far greater variety of climate than does the Golden State. Japan's northernmost main island, Hokkaido, has a climate more like that of Alaska—long, cold winters and short, warm summers. Its principal island, Honshu, which includes the nation's capital, Tokyo, experiences hot, steamy summers, beautiful autumns, chilly winters, pleasant springs, and in early summer a fifth season, called *fuyu*, the rainy season. On the western side of Honshu lies the so-called Snow Country, a region that experiences some of the largest recorded annual snowfalls in the inhabited world.

Japan's southernmost island, Okinawa, enjoys a lush tropical climate, much like that of southern Florida. Unlike Florida, however, in late summer Okinawa and much of the rest of Japan suffers a frequent battering from dozens of annual typhoons that whirl through the western Pacific.

Even so, the most notable feature of the environment is not even part of the climate. Japan trembles incessantly and experiences noticeable earthquakes almost daily. From time to time, these earthquakes have reached devastating magnitudes. In 1995 an earthquake in the port city of Kobe killed more than 5,000 people and left over 300,000 homeless. The most famous temblor in modern times struck Tokyo in 1923. Known as the Great Kanto Earthquake, it killed an estimated 140,000 people and left the entire region in a shambles.

The quakes result from the region's geography. Japan's islands are formed from the peaks and plains of a welter of volcanoes that overlie a great fault in the earth's tectonic plates. More than 80 percent of the land comprises uninhabitable volcanic slopes.

That peculiar geography has forced Japan's people to live in crowded villages and cities for much of their history. Over time, many of those municipalities have knitted together to form seamless megacities. Today, about one-quarter of the nation's 120 million people live in the world's largest metropolitan area, formed by the cities of the Kanto plain—Tokyo, Yokohama, Kawasaki, and Saitama. Hemmed in by an arc of mountains and the sea, the cities have blended so thoroughly that only a map can tell you where the boundaries between them lie.

As dramatic as Japan's volcanic landscape may be, it offers few natural resources. There are some coal mines in the north and some iron and tin mines on Honshu and the westernmost island, Kyushu, but for most of their history the Japanese have had to build their homes mainly from wood, heat them mainly with charcoal, and use paper for windows and doors. Even now, lacking oil or natural gas, Japan relies mainly on nuclear power to generate electricity and on imports for its gasoline and other petroleum products.

In pointing out the extremes, it would be easy to distort the picture of ordinary life, which, despite occasional earthquakes and typhoons, can be very pleasant indeed. Japan's heavy annual rainfall makes the lowlands green, fertile, and well suited for farming, especially of rice, the nation's staple crop. A wide variety of fruits and vegetables also thrive in Japan's climate and soil. Historically, its rivers and shores have offered a bounty of fish and mollusks, the main sources of protein for the Japanese. And, practicality aside, Japan's extreme landscapes are some of the most beautiful on Earth.

Importing Culture Wholesale

Like the peak of Japan's tallest volcano, Mount Fuji, the origins of Japan's culture are shrouded in mist. People have inhabited the islands for as many as thirty thousand years, yet the first known attempt at recording history in Japan took place less than thirteen hundred years ago. The reason is simple: The ancient Japanese had no writing system for their language. Written records had to wait until scholars brought the complex Chinese way of writing with ideograms (abstract pictures that represent words) to Japan's imperial court around the middle of the sixth century.

The importation of writing was part of a wholesale borrowing of Chinese culture. It set a pattern Japan would repeat at crucial stages in its history. Many countries have adopted the cultural practices of neighbors, most often as a result of conquest. Japan, which never experienced conquest until 1945, stands alone for its deliberate policy of importing foreign ways and then carefully adapting them to suit domestic culture or policy.

Along with Chinese writing, Japan imported the Chinese ways of operating a bureaucracy, running an economy, and practicing Buddhism. However, this by no means resulted in Japanese society becoming a pale imitation of China. Instead, the cultural practices borrowed from China took on a distinctly Japanese character. Although Japan borrowed China's system of centralized bureaucracy, for example, imperial rule in Japan was counterbalanced by nearly continuous violence among competing warlords.

Buddhism in Japan branched into a variety of sects. Characteristically, Japanese Buddhism tended to sweep aside the Buddha's philosophical insights, concentrating on ritual instead. Japan's Pure Land sect, for example, offers a simple formula for salvation: the continual repetition of the name *Amida Buddha*.

Most famously, the Japanese created Zen Buddhism. Turning their backs on scholarship and rationality, the followers of Zen sought enlightenment through long hours of mind-emptying meditation, unanswerable riddles ("What is the sound of one hand clapping?"), along with extreme self-discipline. Practitioners were known, for example, to meditate cross-legged under a cold waterfall for hours at a time.

This Japanese form of Buddhism, in turn, gave rise to uniquely Japanese traditions. Japan's samurai warriors, for example, incorporated aspects of Zen Buddhism in their own unique extremity: ritual suicide. The slow, painful, and highly formal ritual of *seppuku*, or, less formally, hara-kiri, requires the participant to kill himself by unflinchingly cutting open his belly and then slicing his internal organs. Though not part of the religion, it was closely linked to Japanese Buddhism, with its emphasis on otherworldly salvation. Samurai would undertake *seppuku* to atone for a shameful act (such as the loss of a battle) or as an honorable means of carrying out a death sentence from a superior.

When European traders and missionaries arrived during the mid-1400s, Japan again accepted a variety of foreign practices, such as the art of gunsmithing, but once again the nation firmly stamped its own policy and style on the imports. Samurai continued to wear—and use—their two swords, long and short, but they added elaborately decorated short-barreled rifles to their armaments and plunged into some of Japan's bloodiest civil wars.

Conformity and Isolation

Amidst feudal Japan's violent culture of warlords and samurai, however, there was a moderating influence on the bloodshed, one that persists today. Running counter to the martial spirit was a vague but powerful Japanese concept known as *wa*.

Loosely translated as "harmony," *wa* has been a guiding principle in Japan since at least A.D. 604, when Prince Shotoku gave Japan its original constitution. The first article proclaims the supreme importance of *wa*. To maintain harmony, *wa* demands that Japanese consider the needs of the group ahead of their own and keep their feelings under tight wraps while trying to sense the feelings of those around them. Historically, *wa* has resulted not so much in peace as conformity. A common saying expresses this tendency: "The nail that sticks up gets hammered down."

So distinctive is this way of keeping society in line that the

Japanese have come to think of *wa* as embodying the Japanese spirit. It helps that *wa* is also an ancient name for Japan. There is, however, a double irony here: Prince Shotoku borrowed the concept of *wa* from the teachings of the Chinese philosopher Confucius. And as a name for Japan, *wa* comes from an ancient Chinese stereotype of the Japanese, meaning "dwarf."

Nevertheless, *wa* has become a thoroughly Japanese concept. Aside from helping to keep order and harmony among people living in close quarters, it has played a significant role in promoting the Japanese sense of uniqueness. That deep-rooted belief helps to account for another feature of Japan's tendency toward the extreme. Although distrust of foreigners crops up in every society, the Japanese historically carried it to a remarkable extent.

During the Middle Ages, European sailors and officials calling at Japanese ports were occasionally beheaded to discourage further visits. Even when the Japanese government allowed regular calls by European ships, foreigners were kept within a few port enclaves, and missionaries were closely watched. Eventually Christianity gained a substantial following but ran afoul of Japan's perennial mistrust of foreigners. Christians were persecuted under the reign of the Tokugawa clan, which came to power in 1600. Over the next few decades the religion was officially banned and ruthlessly stamped out. The Tokugawa clan excluded all foreigners from Japanese soil, made it a capital crime for any Japanese to leave the country, and restricted foreign trade to a twice-yearly visit from Dutch ships to a tiny island in the Japanese archipelago. All through the Scientific Revolution, the Enlightenment, the Napoleonic Wars, the African slave trade, and the founding of modern democracy in America, Japan remained in self-imposed isolation.

Japanese Imperialism

When, at last, during the late nineteenth century, American "gun-boat diplomacy" yanked Japan back into the world, the island nation responded with an astonishing overreaction. Urged on by the enthusiastic blessing of the youthful, energetic Emperor Meiji, Japanese rushed out to scour the Western world for know-how and bring back what they took to be the best of everything.

Government policy concerned itself mainly with building up industry, trade, and a modern military. To that end, Japanese investigators studied the British navy and the German army, along with European steel-making and textile production techniques.

But Japanese curiosity went far beyond those government aims. The travelers brought home German beer, French pastry, British top hats and tails, cattle ranches, Impressionist painting, ballroom dancing, classical music—in short, a whole potpourri of European culture. With great skill, the Japanese set about imitating the techniques that made all these possible, and soon Japan had its own breweries, pastry shops, Savile Row tailors, beef restaurants, and concert halls. From America, they imported a sport that eventually became a national obsession and a special link between the two countries: baseball.

In a single generation Japan transformed itself from an almost medieval land, where the only foreign technology was the rifle, to a modern industrial nation with a fledgling parliamentary democracy under the emperor and the most powerful military in Asia.

Europe and the United States were impressed. Neighbors in Asia were dismayed. In reversing its policy of isolation, Japan swung into the saddle of colonialism. In 1904 it won a decisive naval war against Russia over possession of Korea and Chinese territory in Manchuria. Japan went on to colonize Korea in 1910, and eventually to carve out a large portion of China as the puppet state of Manchukuo under Japanese control.

All this took place in the context of Western colonialism, which brought virtually every country in the world but Japan under the domination of Europe and, to a lesser extent, the United States. For the nations that were dominated, the experience of colonialism was often humiliating and, in many instances, brutally oppressive.

The Japanese military and its giant industrial conglomerates pushed colonial oppression in their Asian empire at least as far as any Western power. During Japan's rule over Korea, the people of that country were forbidden to speak or write in their own language. In China, the imperial army's conflicts with hapless Chinese armed forces spilled over into atrocities on a vast scale. Most infamous was the incident known as the Rape of Nanking. On December 13, 1937, imperial army troops, having chased away ragtag Chinese troops, entered the city of Nanking, then the capital of China. The Japanese troops went on a six-week rampage of mind-boggling ferocity against the unarmed civilian population. Thousands of women and girls were raped and then murdered. Thousands of other civilians were publicly beheaded or eviscerated and left to die. Altogether, historians estimate that three hundred thousand Chinese were put to death before order was restored.

Japan's conquest of nearly all of Asia at the outset of World War II only made things worse. The Japanese military showed great contempt for the countries they occupied, routinely humiliating local dignitaries, forcing women to serve as prostitutes for its soldiers, transporting civilians to work as slave laborers far from home, and systematically mistreating vast numbers of prisoners of war.

Through its increasingly brutal conduct against conquered peoples during the rise and fall of its empire, from 1910 until 1945 (when U.S. atom bombs forced its surrender), Japan earned a bitter resentment that continues to smolder today.

Embracing Pacifism

Yet once the U.S. occupation ended in 1952, Japan showed once again its uncanny ability to swing from one extreme to another. With an American-dictated constitution to guide it, Japan became a pacifist nation, with only relatively meager "self-defense" forces under arms. A unique provision of the constitution, known as Article 9, proclaims that Japan forever renounces the right to wage aggressive war. Although a militant wing of the ruling party agitated for a restoration of the military, the vast majority of Japanese citizens remained firmly opposed to rearmament.

In place of military conquest, Japan bent its will toward economic power. In this it was phenomenally successful, and eventually, as its national wealth grew, Japan became the world's leading provider of aid to developing countries.

If Japan has tended to display extreme contrasts in its relations with the rest of the world, the same may be said of its domestic affairs. Japan has tended to alternate for much of its history between tight central control and chaos. Political change has most often come through assassination, revolution, or civil war. It is not so much the level of violence, however, that sets Japan apart. The history of humankind shows no shortage of bloody conflict anywhere. What sets Japan apart is the unwavering formal commitment to monarchy despite nearly constant jousting for power among competing warlords.

Japan's Rough Transition to Democracy

In marked contrast to the refinement of the emperors and their courts, some of Japan's most successful warlords came from extremely humble origins. Oda Nobunaga (1534–1582), sometimes called "the Napoleon of Japan," rose from an obscure family to bring one of Japan's bloodiest civil wars to a close by cunning and ruthless generalship. His successor, Toyotomi Hideyoshi (1536–1598), was little more than an unrefined peasant when he ascended to undisputed power. Yet he promoted the arts, imposed a class system, and honored tradition. The man who followed him, Ieyasu Tokugawa (1542–1616), was also a nobody until he climbed into the ranks of power. Ieyasu cemented in place a rigid system of central feudal rule that lasted well over two centuries. Yet none of these powerful figures ever directly challenged the emperor system or took on a title more distinguished than *military commander.*

Even after Japan began its transition to democracy, this tendency to separate formal and actual power continued. During the Meiji era (1868–1912), Japan took on the forms of a monarchical democracy. It created a parliament and held elections (although the voting public was at first restricted to a relatively small group of men). Throughout this period, however, actual power lay in the hands of the *genro*, or clique of elder statesmen close to Emperor Meiji. Many of the *genro* were cabinet members, some were shadowy powers behind the throne.

After Emperor Meiji's far less commanding son, Taisho, ascended to the throne in 1912, genuine two-party democracy began to take hold. Yet, once again, power eluded the formal figureheads. The military declined to take orders from anyone but the emperor and, in actuality, gave precious little attention to the wishes of a man they claimed was their living god.

The Japanese military's most famous act of defiance was the so-called Manchurian Incident of 1931, in which the imperial army faked an attack on its own railway in order to justify moving farther into Chinese territory. Emperor Hirohito, though displeased, made no move to punish the conspirators. Thereafter, the army's ambitions in Asia could not be restrained.

One might expect that in the postwar era, with the military reduced to a self-defense force and walled off from political influence, a Western-style democracy would have flourished in Japan. Certainly, during the U.S.-led occupation, when the new constitution enfranchised women for the first time, Japanese voters showed enormous enthusiasm for democracy.

Democracy and Equality Grow

The new social order moved dramatically in a democratic direction. Not only was the aristocracy abolished (though the imperial family retained its titles), but a new ethos of equality took hold. "All Japanese men are created equal" might have been the unspoken new motto of the country. The doors to opportunity for advancement opened wide for all those boys who were able to excel in taking college entrance exams. In the corporate and bureaucratic worlds, hierarchy remained but with significant departures. Workers and managers shared the same office spaces, luncheon rooms, and uniforms. In factories, managers took turns on assembly lines. Salaries were graded by rank, but the disparities between frontline staff and upper management were far smaller than in the United States.

Good opportunities for women and for the small and nearly invisible minorities (mainly Koreans and *burakumin*, a traditionally untouchable class), remained elusive, yet overall the perception of an egalitarian, cooperative society grew strong within postwar Japan. In stark contrast to the civil violence of the past, Japan became by far the safest industrialized society in the world. Murders in Japan have numbered in the hundreds annually, whereas in the United States, which has roughly twice Japan's population, murders have claimed tens of thousands of lives a year.

All the same, representative government would take on a unique form in Japan, in keeping with its long-established pattern of figureheads and shadowy powerbrokers. For all but a brief period during the 1940s and another during the 1990s, one party has dominated Japan's parliament for the half-century since defeat in World War II. What is more, the Liberal-Democratic Party (LDP) shows no sign of giving up power anytime soon.

This is not to suggest that Japan has been a sham democracy. Despite widespread discontent with persistent political corruption, the electorate has consistently returned the LDP to power, largely because it appears to have even less confidence in the ability of the opposition parties—mainly Socialists, Communists, Buddhists, and a smattering of liberal parties—to govern the nation. As its name suggests, the LDP is anything but a monolith. In fact, though it began as an amalgam of two parties, it soon evolved into a welter of competing factions. These political "tribes," as they are often called in Japan, constitute the true political competition. Decisions about power-sharing and policies are hammered out among the factions, far from public view.

It is worth noting, however, that change may be in the offing. As Japan struggles to adapt to new realities—economic competition from its Asian neighbors, deep national debt, persistent recession, a rapidly aging population, and rising military threats abroad—a consensus appears to be emerging in Japan that the political system must change, and as of 2003 a reform-minded prime minister has been making efforts in that direction. Whether they can succeed remains an open question.

Contemporary Contrasts

Japan continues to offer the foreign observer a remarkable range of contrasts in almost every conceivable area. No one familiar with the country's history of physical isolation and cultural insularity can fail to be impressed by its remarkable contributions to global affairs. Since its forced reopening during the mid-1800s, Japan has become the world's leading innovator in consumer electronics. It has also exported a great many aspects of its culture, from ramen noodles and sushi on the one hand to karaoke and kabuki on the other. The Japanese have also excelled at many previously "foreign" pursuits. It has produced world-class scientists such as University of Tokyo professor Masatoshi Koshiba, winner of the 2002 Nobel Prize in physics. It has also trained topflight classical musicians, such as Boston Symphony conductor Seiji Ozawa, and international human rights leaders, such as Sadako Ogata, former United Nations high commissioner for refugees. These achievements point to what may be the most significant contrast of all: Japan somehow combines a penchant for rapid change with a deep commitment to tradition. This has created some dilemmas for Japan. For example, its modern economy gives young women the freedom to earn money, travel, and educate themselves. But the traditional disdain for women working outside the home has severely limited opportunities for women to sustain careers. Japanese women have increasingly chosen to postpone marriage and to limit their family size, with the result that Japan's population structure is rapidly changing: Every year, there are tens of thousands of fewer Japanese youths and tens of thousands of more elderly. This demographic change has placed a growing strain on the budget, medical establishment, and pension system. A campaign to encourage motherhood has so far yielded no results. As a recent editorial in a Japanese newspaper put it, the "Japanese will have babies when living is easy."

A different kind of challenge arises from the tension between Japan's contemporary desire to become more influential in regional and world affairs and its deep, mythological belief in Japanese uniqueness. Japan's sense of cultural superiority has made it difficult for Japan to integrate foreign workers in its society or to win the trust of its neighbors and allies. This has led to deep frustration in Japan over a perceived failure to gain respect and power commensurate with its status as the world's second-largest economy.

Shadows of the Past

At the same time, the rapid growth of China's military and warlike threats from North Korea have contributed to rising insecurity within Japan. The result has been a resurgence of nationalism. Anti-Chinese rhetoric has begun to reappear not only in right-wing journals but even in left-of-center newspapers. A cabinet minister has gone so far as to suggest that Japan might have to develop its own nuclear weapons. And many business leaders and politicians on the right are calling for an end to the constitutional restrictions on military action imposed by the postwar constitution.

All this has raised worries that the revival of a martial spirit could lead Japan to swing once again from pacifism to aggression. However, this is by no means certain. Many Japanese, recalling the horrors of war, remain deeply committed to peace. In any event, it is inconceivable that Japan will reestablish its East Asian empire through conquest. China, once weak and divided, now has the world's largest standing army and a suite of modern weaponry, including a substantial nuclear arsenal. Even bankrupt North Korea reportedly has nuclear warheads and long-range missiles. Japan, with its shrinking base of youth, lacks the capacity, let alone the will, to conquer and occupy its neighbors once again.

Fortunately, Japanese history has another lesson to offer. In the tension between tradition and swift change lies one of the nation's greatest strengths: the ability to adapt to new circumstances without losing its national and cultural identity. So, while it remains true that Japan cannot be summed up with a single theme, readers looking for a way to weave together all the essays in this book may want to consider this thread: resilience. That deeply human quality makes the study of Japanese history worth all the effort it takes to comprehend it.

A Note on Japanese Names

In Japan it is the practice to place the family name first, followed by the given name. Many scholars of Japan follow that convention, even when writing in English. In this book, the editor follows the Western convention of placing the family name last but respects the choice of each essayist.

THE HISTORY OF NATIONS
Chapter 1

Ancient Japan

The Founding Myth

BY THE *KOJIKI*

The Kojiki, compiled more than a thousand years ago, is Japan's oldest book. That alone would qualify it as a national treasure, but additionally it contains some of the most important of Japan's founding myths. The book was completed at the direction of the imperial court in A.D. 712. It contains an account of the origin of the gods, the Japanese islands, and the emperors who came to rule them. Together with the Nihon shoki, written a few years later, it portrays the sun goddess, Amaterasu, as the mother of the nation, with the emperor as her direct descendant, and all the Japanese people, in turn, as lesser relations of the emperor. Although most Japanese recognize that myths do not make accurate history, mythology has played an important role in the history of Japan. In this selection from the Kojiki, Amaterasu's brother, Susano, goes on a rampage after winning a contest against her. Amaterasu takes shelter in a cave and throws the world into darkness. It is a legend known to every Japanese schoolchild and helps to account for the strong sense of national unity that the Japanese have traditionally felt.

Susano-o-no-Mikoto, drunk with victory, broke down the ridges between the rice paddies of Amaterasu Ōmikami and covered up the ditches. Also he defecated and strewed the feces about in the hall where the first fruits were tasted. Even though he did this, Amaterasu Ōmikami did not reprove him, but said: "That which appears to be feces must be what my brother has vomited and strewn about while drunk. Also his breaking down the ridges of the paddies and covering up their ditches—my brother must have done this because he thought it was wasteful to use the land thus."

Even though she thus spoke with good intention, his misdeeds did not cease, but became even more flagrant. When Amaterasu

Ōmikami was inside the sacred weaving hall seeing to the weaving of the divine garments, he opened a hole in the roof of the sacred weaving hall and dropped down into it the heavenly dappled pony which he had skinned with a backwards skinning. The heavenly weaving maiden, seeing this, was alarmed and struck her genitals against the shuttle and died.

At this time, Amaterasu Ōmikami, seeing this, was afraid, and opening the heavenly rock-cave door, went in and shut herself inside. Then Takamano-hara (the abode of the heavenly deities) was completely dark, and the Central Land of the Reed Plains was entirely dark. Because of this, constant night reigned, and the cries of the myriad deities were everywhere abundant, like summer flies; and all manner of calamities arose.

Congress of the Gods

Then the eight hundred myriad deities assembled in a divine assembly. . . . They gathered together the long-crying birds of the eternal world and caused them to cry. They took the heavenly hard rock from the upper stream of the river Amenoyasunokawa; they took iron from [the mountain] Amenokanayama. They sought the smith Amatsumara and commissioned Ishikori-dome-no-Mikoto to make a mirror. They commissioned Tamanoya-no-Mikoto to make long strings of myriad *magatama* beads.

They summoned Amenokoyane-no-Mikoto and Futotama-no-Mikoto to remove the whole shoulder-bone of a male deer of the mountain Amenokaguyama, and take *hahaka* wood from the mountain Amenokaguyama, and [with these] perform a divination. They uprooted by the very roots the flourishing *masakaki* trees of the mountain Amenokaguyama; to the upper branches they affixed long strings of myriad *magatama* beads; in the middle branches they hung a large-dimensioned mirror; in the lower branches they suspended white *nikite* cloth and blue *nikite* cloth. These various objects were held in his hands by Futotama-no Mikoto as solemn offerings, and Amenokoyane-no-Mikoto intoned a solemn liturgy.

Amenotajikarao-no-Kami stood concealed beside the door, while Amenouzume-no-Mikoto bound up her sleeves with a cord of heavenly *hikage* vine, tied around her head a head-band of the heavenly *masaki* vine, bound together bundles of *sasa* leaves to hold in her hands, and overturning a bucket before the heavenly rock-cave door, stamped resoundingly upon it. Then she became divinely possessed, exposed her breasts, and pushed her shirt-band down to her genitals. The Takamanohara shook as the eight-hundred myriad deities laughed at once.

The Sun Goddess Emerges

Then Amaterasu Ōmikami, thinking this strange, opened a crack in the heavenly rock-cave door, and said from within: "Because I have shut myself in, I thought that Takamanohara would be dark, and that the Central Land of the Reed Plains would be completely dark. But why is it that Amenouzume sings and dances, and all the eight-hundred myriad deities laugh?" Then Amenouzume said: "We rejoice and dance because there is here a deity superior to you." While she was saying this, Amenokoyane-no-Mikoto and Futotama-no-Mikoto brought out the mirror and showed it to Amaterasu Ōmikami. Then Amaterasu Ōmikami, thinking this more and more strange, gradually came out of the door and approached [the mirror].

Then the hidden Amenotajikarao-no-Kami took her hand and pulled her out. Immediately Futotama-no-Mikoto extended a *sirikume* rope behind her, and said, "You may go back no further than this!" When Amaterasu Ōmikami came forth, Takamanohara and the Central Land of the Reed Plains of themselves became light.

At this time the eight-hundred myriad deities deliberated together, imposed upon Susano-o-no-Mikoto a fine of a thousand tables of restitutive gifts, and also, cutting off his beard and the nails of his hands and feet, had him exorcised and expelled with a divine expulsion.

Prehistory and the Jōmon Era

By Kenneth G. Henshall

Historians generally rely on the writings of earlier people to carry out their craft. In Japan, however, writing was only imported in about the sixth century A.D. That presents a challenge for recording the lives of people who lived there for many thousands of years prior to that time. To meet the challenge, historians have relied on archaeologists to dig up objects left behind by ancient people. An American scientist, Professor Edward S. Morse, began this work in Japan in 1877, when he discovered ancient pottery buried among discarded seashells. Since then, Japanese archaeologists have uncovered a fascinating and still somewhat mysterious record of the ancient Jōmon pottery makers. Their pots were used for lamps, rituals, food storage, and even the burial of the dead. In the essay that follows, historian Kenneth G. Henshall of the University of Waikato in New Zealand describes the ancient Japanese, from the earliest signs of human habitation of Japan until A.D. 300.

No one is quite sure when the first humans appeared in Japan. Claims have been made for a date as far back as 500,000 years, and some even expect a history of a million years to be proven in due course. The general agreement at present allows for around 200,000 years, though the earliest definite human fossil remains are only about 30,000 years old.

Until the end of the last glacial period, around 15,000 years ago, Japan was joined to the Asian mainland by a number of land bridges. These were through Sakhalin to the north, Tsushima to the west, and the Ryūkyū Islands to the south. In other words, migration into the area was not difficult. Immigrants arrived in waves, particularly from east and southeast Asia some 30,000 years ago, followed by people from northeast Asia about 14,000 years ago.

It is hard to paint a picture of Palaeolithic (Old Stone Age) life with any certainty. One major difficulty is that much of the coastline of that time is now deep under water. There may have been far more coastal activity than the surviving inland sites suggest. The picture emerging so far is basically one of small and seasonally mobile groups of hunter-gatherers. The hunters targeted not only boar and deer but also big game such as elephant and bison, though these were becoming scarcer in the last Palaeolithic phase due to climatic warming and increased hunting by a growing population. Gatherers searched for a variety of berries and nuts such as hazel.

Extended Families

Palaeolithic groups were made up of a small number of extended families, and totalled between 20 and 150 individuals. Extended families were important for the rearing of children, since many parents were dead before their thirties, and there were many orphaned children needing the protection of the longer-lived among the adults. Although the population was growing it probably never exceeded 20,000.

As nomadic hunter-gatherers most groups had only temporary seasonal bases. However, there was some—but limited—stable settlement towards the end of the period. There was also a degree of specialisation, which led to trading. As early as 20,000 years ago obsidian (volcanic glass valued for tool-making) was traded over at least 150 km. This was almost certainly carried by water, indicating that watercraft were in use from very early times.

Stone Age people are popularly portrayed as cave dwellers. However, at least in the case of Japan, caves seem only rarely to have been used as sites of significant permanent occupation—though quite a large number of caves were used as temporary shelters. The preference for open-space sites suggests the widespread use of artificial shelter, though the nature of this is unclear.

Important Palaeolithic sites include Babadan and Takamori in Miyagi Prefecture, Hoshino in Tochigi Prefecture, Fukui Cave in Nagasaki Prefecture, Nogawa near Chōfu in Tōkyō Prefecture, Iwajuku in Gunma Prefecture, and Minatogawa in Okinawa. Judging by a 155 cm [5'2"] male skeleton excavated at Minatogawa and estimated to be around 17,000 years old, Palaeolithic people in Japan appear to have been small by modern standards but similar to other Palaeolithic peoples elsewhere in east Asia.

Knowledge of Japan's prehistoric past was hampered till after

World War Two by the tendency of Japanese archaeologists to interpret their finds in line with the pseudo-historical accounts in early chronicles such as the *Kojiki* and *Nihon Shoki*. Knowledge of the period is now increasing but much still remains to be discovered. It is still not even clear whether the first inhabitants were *homo sapiens* or the earlier *homo erectus*.

World's Oldest Pottery

Around 13,000 BC pottery vessels appeared in Japan. They are the oldest in the world. They also mark the beginning of the Jōmon period, named after the *jōmon* (cord-pattern) found impressed on much of that pottery.

Pottery vessels might suggest a settled lifestyle. Settlement did increase during the period, especially from around 5,000 BC. Groups also expanded into larger tribal communities. The largest Jōmon village yet discovered, at Sannai-Maruyama in Aomori Prefecture, thrived for about 1,500 years between 3,500 BC and 2,000 BC. It covered almost 100 acres and may have had as many as 500 inhabitants at its peak. It is even seen by some as suggesting that Japan could have been a cradle of early civilisation.

Settlement is also associated with agriculture. Primitive slash-and-burn agriculture may have been practised in the west of the country as early as 5,700 BC, but this remains to be confirmed. Also awaiting confirmation are the remains of what appears to be a prehistoric farming community, unearthed very recently at Bibi in Hokkaidō. Dating back to around 4,000 BC, if confirmed this would be the oldest evidence of real farming in Japan. Rice was introduced into the southwest of the country from the continent towards the end of the period, around 1,000 BC, along with millet and barley, but was not widely grown. When it was, it was in dry-fields or marshes rather than paddies. Prior to these introduced plants the most important cultivated plants were probably the beefsteak herb and barnyard grass.

However, despite the pottery and the occasional evidence of farming, the life of the Jōmon people was for the most part one of hunting and gathering, particularly on the coast. Settlements were typically of a semi-permanent nature, in the form of a base camp in a given area, and had around a dozen dwellings. These dwellings were usually pit-houses with thatched roofs reaching down to the ground.

Inland Jōmon people, using the bow and arrow that appeared

around the same time as pottery, mostly hunted boar and deer. At times they also ate a variety of creatures from frogs to badgers to wolves to the Siberian lion—in fact, seemingly the entire range of Japan's rich fauna. The dog was the only domesticated animal during the period.

Many if not most Jōmon people dwelt on the coast, and became particularly adept at using marine resources, from shellfish to oceanic fish. So well did they adapt to this life that Jōmon skeletons, particularly of the latter half of the period, show development of bony protection for the ear mechanisms, strongly suggesting regular and frequent diving. The reason for this coastal preference was that the warming of the climate around 15,000 years ago, which cut off the land bridges, also meant a warming of the seas and an increase in marine resources. Shellfish in particular became a major food source for thousands of years, as evidenced by huge shell mounds such as at Natsushima near Tōkyō Bay.

The climate started to cool again around 5,000 years ago, and sealevels receded. Greater use was then made of inland resources. However, many Jōmon people returned to the coast within a thousand years or so, despite the still cooling climate. This suggests their preference for the life of coastal foragers and fishers was persistent.

Rice Appears

The introduction of rice around 3,000 years ago was probably from China through Korea, where rice cultivation slightly predates that in Japan, though opinion is divided as to the route. Many present-day Japanese make much of the nation's association with rice and assume it has been grown there from time immemorial, but in fact Japan was the last of the Asian nations to adopt rice cultivation.

It can be misleading to think of the Jōmon period as a single fixed entity, for it contained significant variety, both in terms of region and time. Regional variety clearly reflected local conditions, producing for example subcultures such as that centred on deep-sea fishing on the northeast coast. Variety over time reflected not only the warming and cooling of the climate, but the development of new technology. For example, hempcloth was produced from around 5,000 BC, and lacquerware from around 4,000 BC.

The population also seems to have varied over time, often for reasons that are not clear. Though estimates vary and are really only 'best guesses', it was probably around 20,000 at the start of the period, rose to around 100,000 by about 5,000 BC, leapt up to more than twice that by around 3,000 BC (despite the cooling of the climate), then fell back again to about 100,000 by the end of the period. Moreover, again for reasons that are unclear, by this stage the population was gathered largely in the north and northeast.

Other broad changes over time include a progressive increase in awareness of the supernatural. This brought increased shamanism and ritualism, new burial practices, mysterious stone circles in northern Japan, and figurines that seem to have a supernatural significance. Representations of snakes in some locations suggest snake worship.

The increased importance of religious ritual brought about a need for specialised knowledge of procedure. This in turn would have helped lead to differentiation in levels of status within society. Tribal chiefs too, along with the more capable hunters and producers, obviously enjoyed a higher status than most. However, it remains a contested issue as to whether Jōmon society was mainly hierarchical or egalitarian. It is highly likely that over such a long span of time as the Jōmon period, sundry groups would have migrated into Japan from various points, adding a certain degree of ethnic diversity. The disappearance of the land bridges would not have meant a total severing of links with the mainland. Somebody, for example, introduced rice. The number of these immigrants is open to question, but they were perhaps not very numerous, or at least not very different physically, for there seems to have been a recognisable 'Jōmon type'.

Short and Stocky

Jōmon people as a whole are invariably described as short-statured. There are confusing differences in the heights given by experts, but in general Jōmon males towards the end of the period seem to have been around 157 cm [5'3"] and females 148 cm [4'11"]. These heights contrast with those of the subsequent Yayoi immigrants who arrived around 300 BC and marked a new era. The Yayoi were some 3 or 4 cm [1"–1½ "] taller and little different from their modern Japanese descendants at the start of the twentieth century.

As well as being relatively short in stature, the Jōmon people typically had a stocky muscular appearance. They had heavy skeletons, flattened leg bones, and wide, square faces. In fact, the Jōmon people bore considerable similarity to the present-day Ainu of Hokkaidō. This is not surprising, for studies by physical anthropologists confirm that the Ainu are unmistakably descended from Jōmon people. This sets them apart from modern Japanese in the other main islands, who show greater descent from the Yayoi. It is unclear when exactly they arrived in the country, or even exactly where from, but Ainu certainly have a very great antiquity as inhabitants of Japan.

The Ainu are in effect the original Japanese. For many centuries the Yayoi-derived modern Japanese (known in this context as Yamato Japanese) were to deny this, and to marginalise or even ignore the Ainu. It was not until 1997 that there was official recognition of the Ainu's true status as indigenous Japanese.

We see in the Ainu the Jōmon origins of Japan, but Jōmon Japan was still far from being a nation. The following Yayoi period was to contribute far more to the emergence of Japan as we know it today.

The History of Nations
Chapter 2

The Medieval Era

Feudal Lords Fight for Power

By Kenneth Scott Latourette

It took a ruthless and cunning dictator to pull together the various warring powers in the twelfth century. Such a man emerged in Yoritomo, founder of the Minamoto dynasty. He proved his ruthlessness by murdering his brother, Yoshitsune, to take power. He proved his cunning by leaving the emperor and his court in place and setting up a parallel administration in Kamakura, along the coast south of what is now Tokyo.

However, the dynasty did not last long, and, as Kenneth Scott Latourette describes, Japan gradually slipped into anarchy, leading to all-out civil war in 1467. It was a condition that would prevail until the late sixteenth century, when three successive warlords, each building on the accomplishments of the last, forcibly united the country.

It now became the difficult task of the new military leader and dictator, Yoritomo, to organize his power so that it would remain in the hands of his family. He made peace with the powerful Buddhist monks and restored to the civil nobility lands which had been lost during the long wars. He did not attempt to take the imperial throne, nor even to remove the Fujiwara nobility from their offices. He preserved the court at Kyoto. It was still in theory the source of all power in the state, and it was encouraged to maintain its ceremonies. Yoritomo made it useless, however, by establishing side by side with the older civil officialdom a military administration loyal to himself. He appointed, in all the provinces, military constables and military tax-collectors. They did not displace the regular local officials appointed by the civil government at Kyoto, but shared and took over their authority and transacted official business with greater promptness and efficiency. Taxes were levied on all lands

Kenneth Scott Latourette, *The History of Japan*. New York: The Macmillan Company, 1968.

but those of the religious orders: the great estates of the princes were not, as during the later years of the Fujiwara, exempted from these burdens.

Yoritomo Becomes Shogun

This military organization was called the *Bakufu*, literally "tent office." Yoritomo was its head, and in 1192 was given the title of "shogun." Strictly speaking the word "shogun," meaning "general," was not new but had for some time been a common name for military officers of the highest rank. It now took on a new significance, that of the "military dictator." The center of the *Bakufu* Yoritomo removed to the north to Kamakura, not far from the present Tokyo, where he established a separate capital. Kamakura was far from the luxury of Kyoto and from the plots of the court nobility. It was also nearer the military principalities of the north on whose support it chiefly depended.

Thus there came to be two administrative systems, the one civil, the other military, each with its own organization of officials, and each with its capital. The military, at Kamakura, of course, was the stronger, although theoretically it was under the civil. Of the elaborate organization copied from China in the seventh and eighth centuries little remained. Yoritomo must be ranked as one of the greatest political geniuses of his nation, for the dual form of government that he began lasted until past the middle of the nineteenth century, a period of more than six and a half centuries.

Yoritomo's descendants were unable long to retain the control of the machinery that he had so carefully put in operation. His house speedily suffered the fate that had befallen both the imperial and the Fujiwara families. The real power now fell into the hands of the Hojo family. The able head of that house never took over the shogunate, outwardly retaining for the position the same reverence that the Fujiwara had observed toward the institution of the emperor. The office was kept in the hands of minors, however, whose retirement was forced when they approached maturity. At first the office was reserved for the heirs of Yoritomo, but as his direct line died out, descendants of the Fujiwara or of the imperial family were appointed. The heads of the Hojo were content with the title of "regent." They wielded their power with relentless energy and controlled emperors and shoguns with an iron hand.

The Hojo era, in spite of civil strife and military rule, was not without progress in culture and art. New sects of Buddhism arose, the expression of fresh needs and of originality in religious thinking. Like the earlier divisions of Buddhism . . . most had their origin outside Japan and were brought in from China. They were modified, however, by their Japanese adherents. One of these, Zen Buddhism, had a great influence over the military class. Enlightenment was to be obtained not primarily from books, but as Gautama had found it, through meditation.

Zen Buddhism

Zen demanded of its followers a type of intense mental concentration; to know truth one must learn to look at the world from an entirely new angle, and become indifferent to the hardships of life. Zen encouraged simplicity and symbolized through it the deepest meanings. It valued reserve, a perfect self-control backed by concentrated energy. Its sternness and its simplicity were in contrast to the softer teachings and ornate temples of the older sects. It impressed mightily the warrior class and while only a few practiced fully its exacting, rigorous methods, it had a great effect upon feudal life. Painting, architecture and landscape gardening, social intercourse and etiquette, literature, all showed its influence, particularly in the later feudal ages.

As time went on Kamakura, the military capital, began to take on an air of luxury and refinement. Magnificent temples were erected. Tea was introduced from China and with its use there began an elaborate ceremony of tea-drinking closely associated with the Zen sect. With tea came porcelain utensils from the continent, and in the attempt to copy them the Japanese for the first time began to produce superior pottery of their own. Sculpture flourished, especially in wood. Some specimens bear comparison with the best of the work of the Western world. Swordmakers raised their handicraft to the rank of a fine art. Two notable schools of painting developed.

Once during the period Japan was seriously threatened by foreign invasion. The Mongols, a Central Asiatic people, overran Central and Western Asia and Eastern Europe, and established themselves on the throne of China. In the latter part of the thirteenth century their emperor of China, Kublai Khan, decided to attempt to take over Japan. Against the threatened invasion the Japanese united as one people, forgetting for a time their divisions. It took all their strength to repulse it. They were aided by the elements. Storms destroyed the fleets which bore the invading armies. Thus Japan remained the one civilized state in the Far East that had successfully resisted the Mongol arms.

The Ashikaga Period

In time the power of the Hojo was weakened. The defeat of the Mongol invasion strained their resources and the luxury of the life at Kamakura did its work. The regents became corrupt and followed the evil custom of retiring early in life, each in turn leaving his position to a child who was controlled either by his ministers or by an ex-regent. The government presented the sorry spectacle of a puppet guardian of a puppet shogun who was in turn the agent of a puppet emperor. Mismanagement followed. When dissatisfaction was at its height the emperor made a desperate effort to regain the substance of the power whose shadow he enjoyed in the form of reverence in the eyes of the masses, and to end the dual government. Years of civil war followed. Aided by one of the military families, named Ashikaga, the emperor finally prevailed. However, all was not serene and for over half a century civil war was kept up. Private feuds added to the disorder and for a time all centralized authority seemed to be doomed before a reconciliation, with the Ashikaga in power, was reached.

The two centuries (1392–1603) that followed were not destined to be peaceful. The habit of disorder had become too firmly fixed during the years of civil strife to be quickly overcome. The power of the individual military families grew, and away from the immediate vicinity of Kyoto, where the Ashikaga shoguns had located their capital, each was erecting for itself what was practically an independent domain. The powerful chiefs had their *samurai* (warriors) whose contempt for death, ruthlessness, cunning in warfare, and absolute devotion to a chief are seen in modern Japan.

Disorder extended even beyond the bounds of the empire. Daring Japanese merchant pirates harassed the shores of China, plundering and burning cities and towns, avenging the invasion of the Mongols and the failure of the Chinese to grant satisfactory trading privileges. They raided such centers as Ningpo, Shanghai, and Soochow and extended their operations to the Philippines, and to Siam, Burma, and India. For a time it seemed that the Japanese might anticipate by three hundred and fifty years their commercial development of the twentieth century. Internal disorder was increased by Buddhist warrior-monks. Monasteries had grown rich on the gifts of pious emperors, shoguns, and nobles, and sometimes housed groups of thousands of trained fighters. In the years of disorder many of the inmates of these religious houses had armed themselves. More than frequently men assumed the robes of the priest for other than religious reasons and in time the greater monasteries had become the home of desperadoes who terrorized the surrounding country. The anarchy (disregard of government) was still further increased by the extravagance of the Ashikaga shoguns. They had fallen victims to the luxury and vices traditionally associated with the imperial court. Their excesses had necessitated the levy of burdensome taxes. The military families, as their power grew, contributed less and less to the national treasury, and the burden of supporting the state fell on a narrowing region around Kyoto. The load finally became unbearable and the people rose in riots, refusing to pay taxes and asking that all debts be cancelled. The emperors were in dire distress. One Ashikaga shogun brought down on his head the curses of all future Japanese patriots by acknowledging the overlordship of China and accepting from its emperor the title of "King of Japan" in return for trading rights which added to his revenue.

European Complications

The anarchy was further increased by the arrival of Europeans. The explorations of the Portuguese in the age of discoveries, during the fifteenth and early sixteenth centuries, so familiar to all students of Western history, had finally brought them to Japan. Europe had probably first heard of the country from the Venetian traveler, Marco Polo, who had spent some years at the court of Kublai Khan at the time the Mongol expeditions against Japan were being organized. He brought back to Europe marvelous tales of the riches of the islands, and it was partly the hope of rediscovering the country that led Columbus to undertake his famous search for a direct Western route to the East. It was in 1542, nearly fifty years after Vasco da Gama rounded the Cape of Good Hope, that the Portuguese reached Japan, the first Europeans to view its shores. The Spaniards, Dutch and British followed. They established commerce and brought with them two things which were to affect profoundly the future of the nation—firearms and Christianity. . . .

What with the rivalries of the military chiefs, the Buddhist warrior-monks, the weakness of the central government, the anarchy at the capital, the introduction of firearms, and the divisions caused by Christianity, it seemed for a time that the nation might break up. . . .

THE WAY OF THE WARRIOR

For many centuries, the samurai played a large role in Japanese culture, politics, and thinking. In this excerpt from Tsunemoto Yamamoto's 1716 classic, Hagakure, *the self-sacrificing spirit of the bushidō, or "way of the warrior," is revealed.*

The Way of the Warrior (*bushidō*) is to find a way to die. If a choice is given between life and death, the samurai must choose death. There is no more meaning beyond this. Make up your mind and follow the predetermined course. Someone may say, "You die in vain, if you do not accomplish what you set out to do." That represents an insincere approach of the Kyoto people to the *bushidō*. When you are forced to choose between life and death, no one knows what the outcome will be. Man always desires life and rationalizes his choice for life. At that very moment, if he misses his objectives and continues to live, as a samurai he must be regarded as a coward. It is difficult to draw an exact line. If he misses his objectives and chooses death, some may say he dies in vain and he is crazy to do so. But this must not be regarded as a shameful act. It is of utmost importance for the *bushidō*. Day and night, if you make a conscious effort to think of death and resolve to pursue it, and if you are ready to discard life at a moment's notice, you and the *bushidō* will become one. In this way throughout your life, you can perform your duties for your master without fail.

David J. Lu, *Japan: A Documentary History*. Armonk, NY: M.E. Sharpe, Inc., 1997.

Central Government Reestablished

In addition, out of the anarchy of these years arose the men who were to form Japan into a strong centralized state and eliminate internal strife—vigorous leaders who made the modern Japan of today possible. Birth counted for less than it had in some previous centuries, and the man of merit and ability had a much better chance of recognition than he would have had in peaceful times. Members of the lower orders of the military class arose and struggled to establish their supremacy. Three of these stand out as successive masters of the nation—Nobunaga, Hideyoshi, and Iyeyasu. The last was to organize a form of government that was to endure until past the middle of the nineteenth century.

The first of these, Nobunaga, rose through a series of successful wars with his neighbors and made himself master of Kyoto. After serving the shogun for a while he supplanted him. From that time his life was largely a series of wars waged to maintain his position. After his death he was followed by Hideyoshi, who is one of the most remarkable men that Japan has produced, and has at times been called its Napoleon. He was of humble birth, not being even of warrior *(samurai)* rank. Iyeyasu, for a time his enemy, soon allied himself with him, and became his chief lieutenant. Hideyoshi is the one instance in the nation's history of the rise of a commoner to the highest position open to a subject.

After subjugating the nation Hideyoshi gave himself to the task of unifying and increasing his power. Not content with controlling Japan, he dreamed of foreign commercial and political expansion. Near by was Korea, and Hideyoshi planned to reduce it and use it as a gateway for the conquest of China. War was declared and carried on with a cruelty which won for the Japanese the long-lasting hatred of the Koreans. The invasion also involved the islanders with China, who claimed the peninsula as a vassal state and felt that its possession by an alien power would be a menace to her borders. The prolonged attack was only partially successful. Finally, after the death of Hideyoshi, Japanese power in the peninsula dwindled. Iyeyasu by intrigues removed the son of Hideyoshi and made himself master of the country. Slowly the quarreling feudal chiefs were crushed and the authority of the central government was reestablished.

Europeans Reach Japan

By Ian Nish

In the sixteenth century, after many decades of bloody civil war, three successive warlords returned Japan to central control. First, an obscure warrior named Nobunaga defeated his rivals. After his death in 1582, one of his generals, Toyotomi Hideyoshi, took power and grew confident enough to become a patron of the arts and to launch an ill-fated invasion of Korea. The third in this line of strongmen was Ieyasu. During this tumultuous time, Europeans first arrived in Japan, bringing with them trade and Christianity. In this selection, historian Ian Nish examines the role of the new religion in Japan, focusing on how competition between Buddhism and Christianity became one of the battlegrounds in Japan's lengthy civil war.

In 1543 a group of Portuguese sailors had been carried in a storm to Tanegashima in south Kyushu. This was followed by the visit of Francis Xavier, who had already established a great reputation for his work in Goa [in India]. He sailed from Malacca in 1549 in a Chinese junk, owned by one of the buccaneers of the China coast. He had an audience with the daimyo of Satsuma, the modern prefecture of Kagoshima in south Kyushu, but his stay there was unrewarding. Impressed with the scope for evangelism, he went north to Hirado in north-west Kyushu where he had greater success and, filled with enthusiasm, he made the long three months' journey to Kyoto in the hope of meeting the 'king'. When he reached the capital, it was in the throes of civil war, and he was unable to meet either the shogun or the emperor. His mission returned to west Japan where it made some converts. Xavier left for India again in 1551.

The Portuguese traders received an unexpectedly warm wel-

Ian Nish, *A Short History of Japan*. New York: Frederick A. Praeger, Inc. 1968. Copyright © 1968 by Ian Nish. All rights reserved. Reproduced by permission.

come. The local rulers in Kyushu, who were opposed to No-bunaga, were prepared to encourage Portuguese ships to enter their harbours for the sake of the goods they brought, including cannon and gunpowder. The lords deduced that, if they could once learn these skills, they could resist the pressures which Nobunaga sought to impose on them. Correspondingly Nobunaga himself showed a keen interest since the Portuguese goods and skills could confer benefits on his troops.

Christianity Spreads

The appeal of Christianity, which came along with the trade, was just as great and surprising. The daimyo, who wanted trade, were tolerant towards the religion which accompanied it. For long Buddhism had been criticized for its opulent ways, its moral shortcomings and its unscrupulous political involvements. It was ripe for reform; and many saw Christianity as a reformed ascetic doctrine of Buddhism. Christianity was even popular with Nobunaga who was then involved in battles with the Buddhists; he frequently found it necessary to fight the armies of the priests and deprive the monks of their wealthy estates. As part of his policy of clipping the Buddhists' wings, he was sympathetic towards the Catholic priests. In this respect the coming of the Jesuits was well timed. Much was also due to the dominant personality of Xavier whose sincerity and political insight make him one of the important figures of missionary history. He ensured that the Jesuits followed up his pioneering efforts.

From 1560 onwards a band of Jesuits concentrated its energies on Kyoto, the centre of Japanese Buddhism. Nobunaga, who had by 1567 restored order in the area, took the Jesuits under his patronage and conferred on them a lease of land in Kyoto. The attitude shown by Nobunaga operated more widely in their favour. By 1579 the number of converts was about 130,000, who lived mainly in west Japan. In Bungo (Yamaguchi), Arima and Tosa (Kochi), the rulers themselves adopted Christianity as well as most of their subjects. The Jesuit policy of concentrating on the rulers and the educated classes and attaining through them mass conversion of their feudal subordinates had reaped a rich harvest.

This favour continued under Hideyoshi, who was initially hostile to the Buddhist monks and their political alliances. But in 1587, when he was in Kyushu suppressing revolts, he issued edicts ordering the Jesuits to quit Japan within twenty days but permitting Portuguese trade to continue. Here he had misapprehended the temper of the foreigners. Henceforth it was by no means unusual for local rulers when they closed churches and drove away foreign priests to find that the captain of a Portuguese ship refused to trade with them. In this way they were tactfully persuaded to reopen the churches.

The more successful Christian work was, the more it was re-

ST. FRANCIS XAVIERÊS OBSERVATIONS ON THE JAPANESE

Francis Xavier, a Catholic priest and missionary who was later canonized as a saint, introduced Christianity to Japan in the mid-1500s. Here, he records his views of the Japanese.

The Japanese have a high opinion of themselves because they think that no other nation can compare with them in regard to weapons and valor, and so they look down on all foreigners. They greatly prize and value their arms, and prefer to have good weapons, decorated with gold and silver, more than anything else in the world. They carry a sword and dagger both inside and outside the house and lay them at their pillows when they sleep. Never in my life have I met people who rely so much on their arms. They are excellent archers and fight on foot, although there are horses in the country. They are very courteous to each other, but they do not show this courtesy to foreigners, whom they despise. They spend all their money on dress, weapons, and servants, and do not possess any treasures. They are very warlike and are always involved in wars, and thus the ablest man becomes the greatest lord. They have but one king, although they have not obeyed him for more than 150 years, and for this reason internal wars continue.

David J. Lu, *Japan: A Documentary History.* Armonk, NY: M.E. Sharpe, Inc., 1997.

garded with suspicion. What had caused the *volte face* [about face] on the part of Hideyoshi was the fear that the Christian clans of Kyushu were being armed by the Portuguese in order to resist his own centralizing authority. He had found that Nagasaki was full of churches and church-schools and resembled a foreign enclave on Japan's soil. Just as restrictions had earlier been placed on Buddhism, so controls had now to be applied to Christianity when it threatened to become a divisive force. Hideyoshi therefore took steps to enforce his edict only in Kyushu—his 'Christian island'—and only if the Jesuits were obtrusive. The fathers agreed to stop preaching in the open and celebrated the mass in the houses of their converts. They continued to publish in Nagasaki their manuals and their Latin-Japanese dictionaries.

This happy outcome was complicated by the arrival in Japan of the Franciscans from Manila in 1593. They refused to be bound by restraints and claimed that, if they were hindered in public observances, they would be swiftly followed by a naval expedition from the Philippines. The threat of a naval attack was dangerous for Hideyoshi who decided to enforce the edict. In 1597 he undertook persecution of 25 Christians, including 6 Franciscan fathers and native priests in Nagasaki, by cutting off their ears and noses and then crucifying them. These rigorous methods were not much more severe than those applied by the Christian daimyo towards Buddhists or than those applied in the Counter-Reformation in Europe. In the following year Hideyoshi died; and foreigners, who were on the point of leaving, stayed on in the hope of better days ahead.

The Jesuits offered opportunities for their converts to see something of the wider Church. They persuaded three lords of Kyushu—Otomo, Omura and Arima—to send messengers to Rome in 1588–91 under Father Valignano. The messengers were received in audience by the Pope and had an extended journey in Spain and Portugal of which they have left several chronicles. But they were young men of little standing within their clans. Later in 1615 a further embassy from the daimyo Daté of Sendai went to Rome. It is likely that it was one of the motives behind this mission to inquire into improving trade, not so much with Europe as with Mexico and the Spanish possessions in South America.

Japan Closes Its Doors

By Kenneth G. Henshall

At the beginning of the seventeenth century, the succession of generals gave way to a dynastic form of government. The man responsible was Ieyasu. In 1600, having vanquished those who wanted to anoint the son of the late ruler, Hideyoshi, in a battle at Sekigahara, Ieyasu consolidated all power in his hands. In short order, he shifted the seat of government to Edo (now Tokyo) and there founded the Tokugawa dynasty, which was to last more than 250 years. That staying power relied on a rigid and often brutal system of control. As historian Kenneth G. Henshall vividly describes, to ensure their complete domination, the Tokugawas took the extraordinary step of banning Christianity, expelling all foreigners, and sealing off the island nation from the world.

Ieyasu was determined to capitalise on his victory at Sekigahara, and more generally on the accomplishments of Nobunaga and Hideyoshi. His main aim was to ensure the Tokugawa stayed in control of the nation. In this, he would be aided by his survival skills.

In some ways like the nation as a whole, Ieyasu owed much to a mixture of determination, pragmatism, astuteness, and good fortune. A remarkable survivor living in dangerous times, his life is the stuff of adventure stories and films.

He was born Matsudaira Takechiyo in 1542 in Mikawa Province (part of present-day Aichi Prefecture). His mother was just 15 years old and his father, the minor chieftain Matsudaira Hirotada (1526–49), just 16. The Matsudaira family were having trouble with their neighbours, the Oda to the west and the Imagawa to the east. They entered into an uneasy alliance with the Imagawa, and in 1547, to underpin this, Hirotada agreed to send them his young son Takechiyo as hostage. However, while on his way to the Imagawa base at Sunpu (Shizuoka), Takechiyo was captured by Oda forces and taken to the Oda base at Nagoya. Upon his father's death in 1549 a truce was declared between the Oda and Matsudaira families, and Takechiyo resumed his role as hostage to the Imagawa.

Takechiyo stayed with the Imagawa till 1560, seemingly quite settled. While with them he married and became a father in his teens, like his own father before him. He even fought with the Imagawa in their battles. Then in 1560 Imagawa Yoshimoto, the head of the family, was defeated and killed by Oda Nobunaga in the Battle of Okehazama. Takechiyo—now known as Motoyasu—was freed from his vassalage, and in fact became an ally of Nobunaga.

Name Change

With the western borders of his home (Matsudaira) territory now secure through this alliance, Motoyasu turned his attention to the Imagawa territory to the east, and gradually achieved control of this by 1568. By this stage he had changed names again, to Tokugawa Ieyasu. In 1570 he moved his base to the former Imagawa stronghold in Shizuoka, and over the next decade, using his alliance with Nobunaga, was able to extend his territory. At times Nobunaga had doubts about his loyalty, but Ieyasu overcame these. In 1579 he had his own wife and first son—whom Nobunaga suspected of colluding with his old enemy the Takeda family—killed as evidence of his loyalty.

When Nobunaga died in 1582 Ieyasu made use of the ensuing turmoil to occupy Takeda territory in the provinces of Kai and Shinano (present-day Yamanashi and Nagano Prefectures). He was now a major force for Nobunaga's successor Hideyoshi to reckon with.

In 1584 Ieyasu tried to challenge Hideyoshi's authority, but failed, and the following year acknowledged Hideyoshi as his overlord. They then formed an uneasy alliance, which in 1590 helped overcome the Hōjō in the Kantō region (unrelated to the earlier Hōjō). Hideyoshi rewarded Ieyasu with territory taken from the Hōjō, but, still concerned about his loyalty, obliged him to take up this territory at the expense of his existing territory. Ieyasu had little choice but to agree. However, instead of moving into the Hōjō's former base at Odawara, he chose instead the little fishing village of Edo, which was more centrally located within the territory. This obscure little village was later to become one of the world's largest cities and major economic capitals, Tōkyō.

Over the next few years Ieyasu consolidated his huge holdings, which in effect comprised all the Kantō Plain. Among other things he built Edo Castle, which was later to form the foundations for the Imperial Palace. He was acknowledged by many *daimyō* [feudal lords] as their overlord, and felt strong enough to break his promise to the dying Hideyoshi to safeguard Hideyoshi's infant heir Hideyori. Having triumphed at Sekigahara in 1600 he was effectively the greatest power in the land.

Call Him Shogun

To legitimise his position, in 1603 Ieyasu received the title of shōgun [military ruler]—unused since 1588—from Emperor Go-Yōzei (r. 1586–1611). He was now 61 years old. In the manner

---

EDICT OF 1635 ORDERING THE CLOSING OF JAPAN

Starting in 1633, the Tokugawa shogunate began issuing a series of orders to isolate the country. Here is an excerpt from one of their edicts.

1. Japanese ships are strictly forbidden to leave for foreign countries.

2. No Japanese is permitted to go abroad. If there is anyone who attempts to do so secretly, he must be executed. The ship so involved must be impounded and its owner arrested, and the matter must be reported to the higher authority.

3. If any Japanese returns from overseas after residing there, he must be put to death.

4. If there is any place where the teachings of padres (Christianity) is practiced, the two of you must order a thorough investigation.

5. Any informer revealing the whereabouts of the followers of padres (Christians) must be rewarded accordingly.

of earlier emperors and shōguns, just two years later he resigned in favour of his son Hidetada (1579–1632). Though Hidetada was no infant, Ieyasu himself continued to wield actual power. By this early abdication Ieyasu helped ensure the continuity of his line—a continuity further helped by Hidetada's own similar abdication in 1623.

Hideyori was still a potential threat. It took Ieyasu some years, but in 1615 he finally managed to destroy Hideyori's base at Osaka Castle. Still only 22, Hideyori committed suicide when defeat was imminent. His captured 7-year-old son Kunimatsu was executed by beheading.

The same year of 1615, Ieyasu also issued sets of laws to control both the court and the military houses. Though the court had legitimiséd Ieyasu's own position and he treated it with some respect, he made it clear that its authority was merely formal and ceremonial. It was made subject to the control of the shōgunate,

---

If anyone reveals the whereabouts of a high ranking padre, he must be given one hundred pieces of silver. For those of lower ranks, depending on the deed, the reward must be set accordingly.

6. If a foreign ship has an objection [to the measures adopted] and it becomes necessary to report the matter to Edo, you may ask the Ōmura domain to provide ships to guard the foreign ship, as was done previously.

7. If there are any Southern Barbarians (Westerners) who propagate the teachings of padres, or otherwise commit crimes, they may be incarcerated in the prison maintained by the Ōmura domain, as was done previously.

8. All incoming ships must be carefully searched for the followers of padres.

9. No single trading city . . . shall be permitted to purchase all the merchandise brought by foreign ships.

10. Samurai are not permitted to purchase any goods originating from foreign ships directly from Chinese merchants in Nagasaki.

David J. Lu, *Japan: A Documentary History*. Armonk, NY: M.E. Sharpe, Inc., 1997.

which reserved the right to approve all court appointments. Military houses were controlled by the enforcement of the status quo, down to fine detail....

Ieyasu clearly believed that enforced stability and orthodoxy were important to continued control. Change was undesirable because it was hard to predict. Mobility was a threat. The more people acted in a settled and prescribed manner, the less of a threat they posed. Failure to act as expected was even punishable by death. Ieyasu is said to have defined 'rude behaviour'—for which a samurai could lop off the miscreant's head—as 'acting in an other-than-expected manner'.

Death of Ieyasu

Ieyasu died of illness the following year, 1616, and was deified as the manifestation of the Buddha of Healing. How much he had healed the nation was a matter of some debate, but he had certainly helped keep it unified.

His policy of orthodoxy and stability was pursued by his son Hidetada and most of his successors, all of whom were Tokugawa. In many cases it was possible simply to build on policies already put in place by Hideyoshi.

The regulations for military families were soon followed by regulations for other classes. These prescribed not only such matters as type and place of work and residence, and type of clothing, but such minute details as what type of present a person of a particular class could give to their offspring of a particular sex and age, what type of food they could eat, and even where they could build their toilet.

Hideyoshi's freezing of the classes was an important means of enforcing orthodoxy and stability. It was now extended to a formal Chinese-inspired hierarchical system known as *shi-nō-kō-shō*, meaning 'warrior-peasant-artisan-merchant', in descending order of status. Peasants ranked higher than artisans and merchants because in Confucian terms they were seen as essential producers. Within each class, particularly the samurai class, there were numerous sub-rankings.

Court nobles, priests, and nuns were outside the classes, while below the classes were two 'outcast' sub-classes, *eta* ('great filth', nowadays *burakumin*, or 'hamlet people'), and *hinin* ('non-persons'). They were engaged either in despised 'impure' activities such as butchering, leatherwork, and burial, or in 'suspicious' activities such as peddling and acting. *Burakumin* continue to this day to be segregated from mainstream society.

Class was in theory determined by birth, and movement between the classes was difficult—though in practice not impossible as is popularly believed. A main division was between the samurai and the non-samurai. Samurai accounted for only about 6 per cent of the population, and included most bureaucrats since in effect that is what they became. Non-samurai were basically divided into those who lived in the country and those who lived in the towns.

Dividing the Land

The Tokugawa also valued Hideyoshi's policy of domain redistribution. The shōgun himself owned about one-quarter of cultivated land, along with major cities, ports, and mines. The remaining land was strategically divided between the 275 or so *daimyō* on the basis of whether they were *shinpan* (relatives), *fudai* (traditional retainers), or *tozama* ('outer *daimyō*' of questionable loyalty). Though numbers fluctuated, typically there were around 25 *shinpan*, 150 *fudai*, and 100 *tozama*.

Nor could a *daimyō* relax after being given a domain (*han*). Although in theory they were allowed considerable autonomy in matters such as taxation rights and internal administration, including law enforcement, in practice they were expected to follow the examples and guidelines established by the shōgunate. In effect, local government became their responsibility, and they had to carry out their responsibilities to the shōgunate's liking. The shōgunate constantly monitored their behaviour. At the least suggestion of insubordination they were punished. In just the first fifty years of Tokugawa rule no fewer than 213 *daimyō*—the great majority—lost all or part of their domain for offences either real or alleged. In the same period 172 new *daimyō* were given domains as rewards for loyal service, there were 206 instances of domains being increased as a similar reward, and on 281 occasions *daimyō* were relocated.

Families Held Hostage

Hideyoshi's practice of keeping the families of potentially troublesome *daimyō* hostage was extended by the Tokugawa into a system known as *sankin kōtai* (alternate attendance). With just a few exceptions, this obliged each *daimyō* alternately to spend a year in Edo and a year in his domain, while his family remained permanently in Edo. The great expense involved in maintaining a residence in Edo as well as in their domain, and in proceeding to and from Edo on a regular basis with the requisite number of retainers, also helped prevent the *daimyō* from accumulating too much financial power. In fact, it consumed around half their income or more. They were also obliged to travel not only on specific dates but also along specific routes, which were always guarded by shōgunate troops.

Other measures taken by the Tokugawa shōgunate to restrict mobility and limit potential instability amongst the general population included:

- checks on land travel, with officially approved travel documents having to be obtained and shown at the barriers between domains;
- a curfew system that prevented people moving around at night without proper authority, especially outside their own town wards;
- the destruction of most bridges, thereby channelling movement and making it more manageable;
- the effective banning of wheeled transport;
- the use of secret police to report on any suspicious movements or happenings.

Hideous Punishments

Punishment for offenders was usually severe, particularly for those in the major towns in territory controlled directly by the Tokugawa. Execution was common for petty theft or even for negligence in letting your own house catch fire—fires being a particular danger to communities of mostly wooden houses. Whole families, and even neighbours, were sometimes executed along with the miscreant, for Hideyoshi's principle of collective responsibility was applied with vigour. In particular, heads of families and neighbourhood associations were held responsible for the misdeeds of their members.

Punishments in Europe at the time were also severe by modern standards, but the severity of those in Japan was enough to shock many European visitors of the day. The Frenchman François Caron, who spent many years in Japan in the first half of the seventeenth century, wrote that:

> Their punishments are rosting, burning, crucifying both

waies, drawing with four Bulls and boyling in Oyl and
Water.

An Italian visitor, Francesco Carletti, remarked:

> . . . many suffered crucifixion on the slightest pretext,
> such as the theft of a radish. . . . . Sometimes also they
> crucify women, with babies at the breast, and leave
> them both to die in agony together. Their punishments
> are indeed extremely cruel, barbarous, and inhuman. . . .

They both omit beheading, which was not uncommon, but
was by no means the final use of the blade on executed commoners. In a practice known as *tameshigiri* ('trial cut'), samurai
tested the efficiency of their swords on the corpses of executed
criminals until, as Carletti observed, 'the wretched body is
chopped into mincemeat, being left there as food for the dogs
and the birds'. A good blade could cut through three corpses in
one blow, with seven the record—and testing was not confined
to corpses.

Honor in Death

Condemned samurai and nobles sometimes suffered a similar fate,
but in most cases were allowed the 'privilege' of committing suicide by ritual disembowelment, known as *seppuku* or *harakiri*
('stomach cutting'). This was a practice that had arisen in the
Heian period and was meant to show the purity of the victim's
soul, which was felt to reside in the stomach. It was by this stage
often ritualised or even tokenised, with the victim's head being
cut off by an honoured friend immediately after the incision.

The severity of the punishments makes an interesting contrast
to the relative leniency of the *ritsuryō* system almost 1,000 years
earlier, and suggests one difference between court rule and martial rule. At the same time, however, punishment continued to be
based on disobedience and disruptiveness, rather than moral
judgement. . . .

Challenge of Christianity

Westerners always presented a problem. They were not familiar
with Japanese ways, behaved unpredictably and often defiantly,
spoke strange languages that were hard to monitor, and had
strange ideas about some divine power that transcended emper-

ors and shōguns alike. Their trade was useful, true, and they had
some useful technology, but they were simply too much of a
threat for the shōgunate's peace of mind. In particular, the challenge that their uncompromising God presented to the authority of the shōgun was a major problem—not so much in theological terms, but political ones.

Had westerners kept their Christian beliefs to themselves, and
not tried to assert the authority of their God—and their God
alone—through preaching and moral judgements, they may well
have received better treatment. Japan was (and still is) a land of
religious tolerance. Nobunaga's campaigns against Buddhist institutions were based on political rather than religious grounds,
and the same was true of the actions by Hideyoshi and then the
Tokugawa against the Christians.

Though the Japanese did not concern themselves overly with
the theological distinction, Catholicism was seen as more of a
threat than the newly emerged Protestantism. This may have been
because Catholics comprised the great majority of the Christians
in Japan—and virtually all the converted Japanese—or because
they were more outward and assertive in the expression of their
faith than the Protestants. Most likely, however, it was largely because the shōgunate was aware of the vigorous empire-building

*The daimō are pictured here, urging the shōgunate to expel the foreigners from
Japan.*

being pursued by Catholic nations in the New World. Columbus himself had come from a Catholic nation. Moreover, the Catholic Church even had its own state, the Vatican, with popes who often became involved in politics. This all clearly suggested that the Catholic Church was not merely spiritual.

In any event, Christianity came to symbolise the western presence and threat to shōgunal power and authority. It became a focal point for shōgunal action against that threat. This action applied not only to westerners themselves, but also to those Japanese who had been converted to Christianity. Like the punishments of the day, it was harsh, particularly against Japanese Christians.

Persecution intensified through the early 1600s. Many suspected Christians were asked to demonstrate their rejection of Christianity by stepping on a copper tablet that bore an image of a crucifix or similar Christian symbol. Some remained steadfast in their faith even though the tortures used to persuade them to renounce it were horrific, including, for example, eye-gouging and the torturing of young children in front of their parents. The executions were similarly horrific, involving methods such as crucifixion, beheading by saw, or throwing into boiling thermal pools.

A Massacre

The culmination of persecution was the Shimabara Massacre of 1638, near Nagasaki, in which as many as 35,000 people—men, women, and children, and most of them Christians—were killed by shōgunate forces. This was not purely a persecution of Christians, but was at the same time the quelling of an uprising partly caused by discontent over taxation and an unpopular *daimyō*. Nevertheless, the causes became conveniently blurred, and it brought an effective end to the open presence of Christianity in Japan (though 'hidden Christianity' was to persist among some, especially in the Nagasaki region). From 1640 all Japanese were obliged to register at Buddhist temples to prove their non-Christianity, a practice which also helped keep a check on the population at large.

Christian missionaries had been expelled in 1614, but western traders had been allowed to continue to visit and even reside in the country. Gradually, however, the shōgunate came to feel that the disadvantages of foreign trade outweighed the advantages. It was not only a constant worry in terms of national security, but a perceived indirect threat to the Tokugawa through the enriching of certain *daimyō* participating in foreign trade. Even at such an early stage, the shōgunate also had an economically motivated wish to preserve domestic merchants from excessive competition.

Closed to the World

By 1639 all westerners had been expelled or had left voluntarily, with the exception of the Dutch, who were allowed only on the small island of Deshima in Nagasaki Harbour. Along with the Chinese and Koreans, they were the only foreigners formally allowed to trade with Japan as it effectively withdrew from the world for the next two centuries. This was the period later described as the *sakoku jidai*, or 'closed country period'.

It was not just a case of foreigners being banned entry into Japan, for the shōgunate seemed to reject almost any form of 'foreignness'. From 1635, with very few exceptions, Japanese were not allowed to travel overseas, and those Japanese who were overseas at the time—who numbered in the tens of thousands, mostly in southeast Asia—were banned from returning on pain of death. The building of large vessels capable of ocean travel had also been banned by that stage. Ships authorised for coastal trading had to display an official shōgunate seal.

The arrival of westerners had helped generate a national consciousness in Japan, aided by the process of reunification that followed shortly afterwards. It was during the 1600s that the Ryūkyū Islands to the south and Hokkaidō to the north began to be incorporated into the nation, giving it a geo-political identity very close to present-day Japan. Japanese world-maps of the time, in another example of adaptation from the Chinese, show Japan—not China—as the centre of the world. Clearly, for the time being at least, Tokugawa Japan was not interested in too much involvement with the lesser nations of its world. A closed country was also a much safer country for its Tokugawa rulers.

Life in Tokugawa Japan

By James L. McClain

The Tokugawa shoguns were undeniably rigid, harsh, and brutal, but they did succeed in bringing peace and stability to Japan. Furthermore, by requiring each region's feudal lord to spend every other year in residence at the capital, Edo (now Tokyo), and by investing in transportation, the Tokugawas contributed to the social and economic integration of Japan. In the selection that follows, historian James L. McClain describes how this resulted in Japan becoming one of the most urbanized and economically sophisticated nations in the world even while it lay in near-total isolation.

About the time that Tokugawa Ieyasu became the shogun of Japan, the Mitsui family decided to pack away its swords and become merchants. For several generations, heads of the Mitsui house faithfully had served the Sasaki daimyo of Ōmi Province, and by the middle of the sixteenth century Mitsui Takayasu, also known by his honorary title of Lord of Echigo, was ensconced in a branch castle near Lake Biwa. When Oda Nobunaga launched his campaign to consolidate control over central Japan in the late 1560s, he obliterated the Sasaki family, and Takayasu beat a quick retreat to the small marketing center of Matsusaka in Ise Province. From that location, Sokubei, Takayasu's son and successor to the family headship, watched the House of Tokugawa rise to a position of military dominance. Sensibly, according to an official family history compiled long after the fact, Sokubei soon concluded that an era of lasting peace was about to settle over Japan, and he further reasoned that the Mitsui family would enjoy a brighter future as shopkeepers than as warriors. Scraping together the necessary capital, he opened a

James L. McClain, *Japan: A Modern History*. New York: W.W. Norton & Company, Inc., 2002. Copyright © 2002 by W.W. Norton & Company, Inc. All rights reserved. Reproduced by permission.

brewery, which he named Echigo Dono no Sakaya (The Lord of Echigo's Sake Shop).

Sokubei's timing was providential, for the sake business brought in enough for the young man to marry and begin to raise a family. He was even more fortunate to take as his wife the young Shuhō, the daughter of a fellow merchant. Wed when she was just twelve years old, Shuhō eventually bore Sokubei a dozen children and still found time to contribute to the family's business success. With an eye to earning more than just an income from brewing, Shuhō persuaded her husband to use some of their savings to open a combination pawnshop-moneylending business. The profits from that endeavor quickly overshadowed the proceeds from the Lord of Echigo's Sake Shop, and the Mitsui family became one of the leading merchant houses in Ise Province.

After Sokubei died in 1633, Shuhō sent her eldest son to Edo with enough capital to open a branch shop. Two years later she dispatched her youngest son, Takatoshi, to assist him, and not long thereafter Takatoshi took over the Edo operations from his older sibling. An adroit businessperson, Takatoshi also became a rice broker and turned the profits from the various Mitsui enterprises into a sizable sum before deciding in 1673 to open a draper's shop in Edo, which he named the Echigoya (The Echigo Shop). At first, this was a small operation, employing a dozen or so clerks who took samples of fine silks to the residences of well-to-do samurai, negotiated a price that varied according to the depth of the customer's purse, and accepted orders on credit.

First Department Store

When a fire destroyed his shop in 1673, Takatoshi reopened the Echigoya at Nihonbashi, where its direct descendant, the main Mitsukoshi Department Store, stands today. There Takatoshi revolutionized retailing practices when he hung out the famous signboard, still preserved in the Mitsui Museum, announcing GENKIN, KAKENE NASHI ("Cash Only, Fixed Prices"). That is, the Echigoya began to carry a line of textiles that ordinary merchant and artisan families, as well as wealthy samurai, could afford, and Takatoshi expected customers to come directly to his store, where they paid cash for goods whose prices were openly advertised and marked the same for everyone. As sales expanded dramatically, Takatoshi spread the Echigoya's fame by lending customers oiled-paper umbrellas on rainy days, each gaily emblazoned with the store's trademark, and by befriending playwrights and poets who furthered enhanced Mitsui's public image in their writings. By 1700 the Echigoya had become Japan's largest store, and Takatoshi had opened branches in Kyoto and Osaka. The Mitsui were not typical merchants; few others could match their successes, and not many family histories accorded their women as many accolades as Shuhō received. Nonetheless, Sokubei was only one of thousands of warriors who chose to become merchants at the beginning of the early modern era, and it was not uncommon for a wife and mother to share the responsibility of running a family business, even though the husband and father stood as the official household head. Together with the Mitsui household, many of those families participated in the three great revolutions that swept across Japan during the early modern era. A country of villages and largely self-sufficient farm families when Ieyasu received his appointment as shogun, Japan within a century became highly urbanized, and countless children of farmers, as well as the offspring of former samurai, moved into the emerging cities in search of better lives as merchants and artisans. There, as they struggled to provide for themselves and hoped even to prosper, they created a commercial economy, as exemplified by the appearance of dry goods emporiums such as the Echigoya. . . .

Osaka Rising

Aware of the military and political significance of the Osaka region, the House of Tokugawa rebuilt the castle to serve as its defense anchor in western Japan. By the end of the seventeenth century, the merchant and artisan population of the surrounding community had soared to approximately 365,000, rendering nearly invisible the 1,000 or so samurai stationed at the castle. As Osaka underwent a metamorphosis from military redoubt into a bastion of commercial activity, it emerged as the country's leading center of production for many goods used in daily life. By 1700 Osaka's artisans were famous for squeezing rapeseeds into lamp oil, fashioning raw cotton into finished cloth, and refurbishing used household goods for resale in secondhand stores. By that date the Sumitomo family and other copper smelters were among the city's largest employers, with seventeen refineries in the city, approximately ten thousand households depended on the copper trade for their livelihoods.

It was inevitable that Osaka, home to so much manufacturing, would become a major shipping and distribution center, a transition encouraged by its proximity to the Inland Sea. By the 1710s more than two thousand ship's carpenters resided in the city, as did thousands upon thousands of wholesalers, distributors, jobbers, and forwarding agents. Somewhat later one respected city official wrote that Osaka "lies at the intersection of the great sea routes of the country and is congested with goods and traffic. Thus, people commonly say that Osaka is the 'country's kitchen,' a storehouse of provisions for all Japan. Indeed, the eaves of the affluent and of wealthy merchant families line the streets of the city, and ships from many provinces always lie at anchor in the harbor. Rice, the necessities of daily life, even goods from abroad; all are

THE GROWTH OF KABUKI

During Japan's isolation, especially during the Genroku period (1688–1703), prosperous merchants patronized a variety of distinctly Japanese arts and entertainments. Among those that flourished during this cultural renaissance were woodcut prints called ukiyoe, *sumo wrestling, and the stylized theater known as* kabuki.

Kabuki was created by Okuni, a shrine maiden in the latter part of the 16th century. Her performances in the dry river beds of ancient Kyoto caused a sensation. Early kabuki consisted mostly of music, acrobatics, dance and mimicry performed by women, most of whom were prostitutes offstage. Finally in 1629 the government banned women from the stage to protect public morals, just one in a long history of government restrictions placed on the theater. This ban on women, which lasted about 250 years until the Meiji Period, necessitated an emphasis on skill over beauty, of drama over dance. Men started to perform female roles, as *onnagata* (female impersonators).

The Genroku Period, the last quarter of the 17th century, marked a cultural renaissance when both aristocratic and common arts flourished. Cut off from the outside world for

brought to this place and put on sale. The people lack nothing." The shogun's direct retainers, the bannermen and housemen, provided the nucleus for Edo's growth. Most of those twenty thousand or so families employed attendants, valets, and households servants, jobs that drew tens of thousands of rural immigrants to the shogun's capital. After Iemitsu institutionalized the system of alternate attendance in the 1630s, the members of the daimyo's immediate families who resided permanently in Edo together with their extensive entourages added perhaps another one-third of a million to the city's population, bringing the total warrior count to approximately 500,000. Like Rome, Edo was built on seven hills, and the elite daimyo located their estates on verdant hillsides that rolled away to the south of the castle. The shogunate

over 50 years, a native stamp was put on many art forms. Many of the most famous *ukiyoe* woodblock prints . . . were designed as posters for kabuki theater. At this time most of the conventions and stylizations of kabuki, entertainment for Japanese townspeople, developed—play structure, character types, the art of the *onnagata*. The playwright Chikamatsu Monzaemon, often called the "Shakespeare of Japan," and actors like Ichikawa Danjuro and Sakata Tojuro left strong legacies that can still be seen today. . . .

Kabuki conventions include use of artificially high-pitched voices, exaggerated gestures, miming, flamboyant costumes, and extreme makeup, but no masks. The beauty of formalization is clear in the acting—the most important aspect of kabuki. When a kabuki actor prepares for a role, he first studies the models perfected by his predecessors. Even if a technique originally represented realistic images, today such technique often seems formalized and symbolic. Thus, even in realistic kabuki, the most trivial gestures are frequently closer to dancing than to acting. Almost every gesture is accompanied by music.

Maria Domoto, "Japanese Civilization and Culture/Performing Arts: Kabuki," course materials at www.uncc.edu (University of North Carolina at Charlotte).

settled its trusted bannermen and their families on Kōjimachi Rise, to the west of the castle. Military considerations entered that decision since the area fronted onto the Musashi Plain, a natural avenue of attack on the castle. Still, the undulating hilltop was considered a choice location since most bannermen could find sunny spots upon which to situate their homes and gardens.

World's Largest City

Throughout the seventeenth century, construction workers, craftspeople, and dealers in all manner of goods poured into Edo to cater to the needs of its burgeoning samurai-administrator population. The heart of merchant Edo was Nihonbashi, about halfway between the shores of Edo Bay and the main entry gate to Edo Castle. From that center, artisan and merchant neighborhoods spread out, nestling in the valleys that twisted through the sunlit hillsides dominated by daimyo estates and samurai residences. By the 1720s, as many merchants and artisans resided in the city as did samurai, and with a total population well in excess of one million, Edo had become the world's largest city.

With Edo leading the way, Japan became one of the most urbanized countries in the world. At the beginning of the early modern era, Kyoto was the only Japanese city with more than 100,000 residents. By 1700 Edo, Osaka, Nagoya, and Kanazawa also exceeded that mark, and approximately 5 to 7 percent of all Japanese lived in such large metropolises. That compared with a figure of 2 percent in Europe, where only fourteen cities were as large, and where only the Netherlands and England-Wales had urban concentrations greater than Japan's. It was a period of urban construction unparalleled in world history, and Japan's remarkable century of urban growth profoundly affected the country's economic and social development.

The robust vitality evident in the Three Metropoles of Edo, Osaka, and Kyoto helped spark a great commercial revolution that swept across the entire country. Although the daimyo and shoguns originally conceived of the regional castle towns and the cities of Edo and Osaka as defensive enclaves, the mass migration of merchants and artisans transformed those communities into pulsating nodes of consumption and production, so that ultimately their commercial significance exceeded by far their original military purpose. In turn, the geometrically expanding volume of handicraft production and trade depended on the development of a highly integrated nationwide marketing system, the elaboration of reliable transportation facilities, and the creation of an infrastructure of banking, insurance, and other business services. Japan entered the early modern period as an agrarian society; by the nineteenth century nearly every Japanese family to some extent was participating in the urban-based commercial economy, and all felt the touch of its consequences.

Ironically, the extraordinary commercial expansion achieved during the era of the Great Peace originated in the crucible of sixteenth-century warfare. Armies required provisions, and even in the midst of widespread destruction and turmoil, farmers sought to boost yields by improving their tools, devising new strains of seeds, and formulating richer fertilizers. At the same time, innovative engineering techniques enabled daimyo and rural communities to undertake major irrigation, flood control, and land reclamation projects that nearly doubled the amount of land under cultivation between 1550 and 1650. The enhancements to the country's productive capacity supported an accelerating growth in population, so that in the century and a half after 1550 the total number of Japanese leaped from approximately ten or twelve million to thirty-one million and simultaneously made it possible for many children to leave the farm and seek their futures as merchants and artisans in the city.

Expanding Trade

The inexhaustible consumption demands of the mushrooming urban population for food, clothing, and building materials stimulated the rapid growth of interregional trade and the development of a nationwide marketing system. Clearly, no one domain could produce all the different goods and foods gobbled up by the residents of its castle town, and it took the entire nation to supply the nearly insatiable appetites of the men, women, and children of Edo and Osaka. Responding to the call of the urban market, producers in different regions became famous for certain specialties: Camphor and shiitake mushrooms from southern Kyūshū, lumber and charcoal from Tosa domain, Toyama medicines, and Kōfu grapes were only a few of the many items that fetched handsome prices in the Three Metropoles.

Daimyo policies contributed to the expanding exchange of goods nationwide. The regional lords needed considerable sums of cash: to keep their castles in good repair and carry out irrigation and land reclamation projects within their own domains, to pay the periodic levies imposed by the shogunate, and to finance their annual journeys back and forth to Edo and to cover the costs of maintaining residential estates and supporting the retinue of relatives and retainers living permanently in the city. Since daimyo derived the overwhelming proportion of their income from agricultural taxes paid in rice, they needed to convert the collected grain into cash in order to pay all the bills that came their way. Beginning in the 1620s, the lords from central and western Japan began to ship their tax rice to Osaka, where rice brokers arranged to have it sold in various urban centers. In the beginning, perhaps one million koku of rice annually passed through Osaka's warehouses, a figure that increased more than fourfold by the 1720s. The flow of such enormous amounts of grain—the nation's principal dietary staple—into and out of Osaka helped transform that city into the economic hub of Japan, the "country's kitchen" in the parlance of the day.

Support of the Overlords

In their quest for revenue, many daimyo eventually enacted policies designed to promote the development of cash crops and local specialty products that could be marketed in consumer centers such as Edo and Osaka. Such schemes assumed a variety of forms. The Maeda daimyo paid a handsome stipend to a famous Kyoto potter to spend a year training local crafts-people at kilns in the villages of snowy Kaga domain. Farther to the north, in Yonezawa, the Uesugi daimyo house brought in experts from other parts of the country to establish indigo plantations, used to produce one of Japan's favorite dyes, and to teach techniques of weaving cotton cloth to local farmers. In the final decades of the eighteenth century, domain officials again invited outside specialists to Yonezawa, this time to advise farmers about planting groves of mulberry, whose tender, young leaves were fed to silkworms. The lord of Yonezawa also funded the establishment of twelve nurseries to propagate mulberry seedlings and published handbooks to teach rural families the secrets of raising and marketing silkworms.

The daimyo hoped to profit from the domain-sponsored enterprises in several ways. In some instances, the officials authorized only certain merchants or villages to participate in the new endeavor and then charged them an annual licensing fee for that privilege. In other cases, the regional lords levied new taxes, such as a set payment for each mulberry tree grown or bale of ceramics shipped out of the domain. In still other instances, officials compelled producers to sell their output to designated wholesalers, who then shipped the goods to dealers in Osaka and turned over a portion of the proceeds to domain coffers. In addition to increasing domain revenues, most daimyo hoped that successful intervention in the economy would work to the advantage of ordinary people and contribute to the perception of benevolent lordship. As one early-nineteenth-century manual on sericulture explained, "The immediate benefit which silk farming brings to society is that it enables unused land along river banks, in the mountains and by the edge of the sea to be planted with mulberries, and silk spinning and weaving to flourish. Needless to say, when the products of the region are exported to other areas, the domain will become rich and its people prosperous."

The shogunate further facilitated the flow of goods across the country by encouraging the standardization of weights and measures and by establishing a national currency. With most of the nation's mines under its control, the shogunate began to operate mints in several cities, and the silver mint, or *ginza*, in Edo reached such prominence that the term eventually became used as the place-name for the section of the city where it was located. Quickly the shogun's coins became the country's currency; while most daimyo issued paper money valid for business dealings within individual domains, merchants calculated payments for commodities that crossed domain borders and for transactions consummated in Edo, Osaka, and other major marketing centers in terms of the gold, silver, and copper coins issued by the shogunate.

Roads and Waterways

The shogunate aided the development of transportation and communication facilities. Since overland transport was difficult in mountainous Japan, most merchants preferred to trust their goods to oceangoing barges and cargo boats. To aid waterborne commerce, the shogunate commissioned Kawamura Zuiken, a wealthy Edo lumber merchant, to institute measures that would reduce existing dangers to coastal vessels. Kawamura immediately set about charting dangerous waters, erecting beacons and lighthouses, and providing lifesaving and rescue facilities from Edo to ports along the northern Pacific coast. He then did the same for the entire coastline along the shores of the Sea of Japan, through the Shimonoseki Strait, and up the Seto Inland Sea to Osaka. When the Kamigata Circuit completed the gap between Osaka and Edo in the 1670s, the so-called Eastern and Western Shipping Circuits linked the most remote regions of Japan to the country's major consumption centers.

The shogunate also undertook a systematic program of road improvement, with an emphasis on the Five Highways that radiated outward from Nihonbashi, the hub of merchant Edo. The most heavily traveled of the great roads was the Tōkaidō, which generally followed the Pacific for nearly three hundred miles from Edo to Kyoto, with an extension continuing to Osaka. The graded roadbed, a deep layer of crushed gravel covered with packed-down sand, averaged nearly twenty feet in width. Markers placed atop mounds planted with pine trees showed travelers how far they had journeyed from Nihonbashi, or how much farther they still had left to go, and stone guideposts kept them from turning the wrong way at crossroads. Strung out along the Tōkaidō Highway were fifty-three post towns where weary travelers could replace their sandals, enjoy a snack and cup of tea, and check into an inn for dinner and a night's lodging. . . .

Japan's commercial revolution changed the face of the country's cities. If the castle towns and the great metropolises of Edo and Osaka began as cities of lords and samurai, by the end of the early modern era they had become the domain of commoners. That transformation can be seen clearly in wood-block prints that celebrated life in the merchant quarters. Hiroshige, often considered Japan's finest print artist, produced more than a thousand scenes of Edo, and he began his most famous work, *Tōkaidō gojūsantsugi* ("Fifty-three Stations of the Tōkaidō Highway") with a view of Nihonbashi, the center of merchant Edo. In similar fashion, popular guidebooks, such as *Naniwa suzume* ("The Naniwa Sparrow") and *Edo meisho zue* ("An Illustrated Guide to Places in Edo"), depicted shops in Osaka and Edo overflowing with customers contemplating the purchases of an almost endless variety of goods.

The History of Nations
Chapter 3

Japan Modernizes

The U.S. Navy Arrives

By Pat Barr

More than two hundred fifty years of enforced isolation left Japan trailing the Western world in many respects. Having allowed only brief visits by Dutch traders to the remote Japanese island of Deshima, it had missed out on the physics of Newton, the music of Mozart, and more crucially the development of naval artillery. That was not its only problem. The Tokugawa dynasty, so ferociously efficient at its outset, had decayed. With other Asian nations coming under European colonial domination, Japan could not avoid being challenged. As it happened, a Western country not known as a colonial power made the first move. In 1852, U.S. president Millard Fillmore instructed Commodore Matthew Perry to lead a fleet across the Pacific and firmly but politely deliver a presidential letter proposing a commercial treaty. The Japanese were astounded by the sudden appearance of the huge, coal-fired naval vessels. Historian Pat Barr tells of the momentous arrival of "the Black Ships" and how they changed Japanese history.

The hot, bright eastern day chosen for the end of Japan's two centuries of seclusion was 8 July 1853. The ships of Commodore Perry's command were black and tall; they were called the *Susquehanna* (the flagship), the *Mississippi*, the *Plymouth* and the *Saratoga;* they had come from China and established a base at Loo-Choo (Okinawa). Their Commodore, Matthew Calbraith Perry, was a big, dark, unsmiling man with a double chin that puffed over the gold braid of his high naval collar. He came from a famous family of hard-drinking, adventure-seeking successful naval officers. Matthew, who was born in 1794, followed in his father's and brothers' footsteps—except that he didn't much like drinking—by becoming a midshipman at the age of fifteen, getting his first taste of battle in the war of 1812 against the British and gaining experience of exotic lands and peoples during his voyages to West and South Africa, Tangiers and the Caribbean.

Rising to Greatness

At the age of forty-six he was made a Commodore and a commodore, wrote one of his biographers, 'was a titanic personage afloat or ashore' who occupied in solitary state the best quarters on the best ship of the squadron and who was surrounded by a retinue of secretaries, body-servants and aides. Perry was a man who gained the respect rather than the affection of those who worked under him and his most sympathetic characteristics were, perhaps, a great sense of fairness and a lively, inquiring mind which recorded all he saw and heard—stories of 'sailing fish', names (ancient and modern) of prevailing winds, fishing techniques of the Malays, colours of rock, bird and native robe. On his expedition to the Far East, Perry's full title was 'Commander in Chief U.S. Naval Forces, East India, China and Japan Seas, and Special Ambassador to Japan'. For Perry had come to demand— not, he made it very clear, 'to solicit as a favour'—that the Japanese should make some kind of trading agreement with America and open at least two of their ports to foreign ships.

In the wood-and-paper village of Uraga, near Yedo [Edo, now Tokyo] before the masts of Perry's squadron appeared on the horizon, life went on as usual. Old men were mending fishing-nets on the beach and women carried wooden buckets of water to the doorstep or clopped along in their high pattens to buy spinach, pickled radish and eels at the shops. In the bay before the village, broad-sailed fishing junks lolloped quietly over the waves.

But, as the strange ships came into view, the fishermen exhibited signs of great consternation. They furled the bellying sails which collapsed in wrinkled, tatty heaps on the decks, they shouted, pulled in their nets with tearing haste, grabbed oars and rowed madly towards the safe shore, 'like wild birds at a sudden intruder', wrote Francis Hawks, Perry's careful chronicler. Ashore too, however, the bright day was shattered and there was panic. Temple bells cried out a bewildered warning and ordinary citizens ran for cover indoors, while the local officials hurried down to the jetty and stared at the black, approaching hulks.

When the ships were within about a mile of Uraga a gun salute was fired and anchors were dropped. Twilight fell with summer suddenness. American sailors, leaning over the ships' rails, watched millions of jellyfish floating in the pale-grey sea, and, as night came, the shore shivered with agitated fires that had been lit on the headlands near the harbour. In Yedo itself every look-out tower was a-twitter with citizens craning their necks towards the dark ocean and every temple was filled with devout old women who clapped their wrinkled hands to call the gods' attention to this disaster and prayed for a tempest that would blow the intruders away. Inazo Nitobe, a contemporary Japanese commentator, wrote, 'The popular commotion in Yedo at the news of a "foreign invasion" was beyond description. The whole city was in an uproar. In all directions mothers were seen flying with children in their arms and men with mothers on their backs. Rumours of immediate action exaggerated each time they were communicated from mouth to mouth and added horror to the horror-stricken. The tramp of war-horses, the clatter of armed warriors, the noise of carts, the parades of firemen, the incessant tolling of bells, the shrieks of women, the cries of children dinning all the streets of a city of more than a million souls made confusion worse confounded.'

To add more terror to that sleepless night, a meteor with a scarlet wedge-shaped tail plummeted down the sky before dawn and the Japanese covered their eyes and bowed their heads with the fear of this baleful portent. But, as the meteor's incandescent light danced briefly over the steel of the foreign ships, Commodore Perry interpreted it quite differently and is recorded as saying that such a phenomenon 'may be so construed by us, as we pray to God, that our present attempt to bring a singular and isolated people into the family of civilised nations may succeed without resort to bloodshed.'

Sketching the Barbarians

At any rate, in spite of the auguries, the Japanese discovered that the world did not end that night and, very rapidly, their naturally courageous curiosity reasserted itself. They decided to inspect the intruders. On the morning of the ninth, several high-prowed little boats bobbed at anchor near the steel sides of the *Mississippi* and the Americans were amazed to see that they were crammed full of artists who, equipped with slender-tipped brushes, ink-stones and rolls of grainy rice-paper, were making hasty—and very lively—sketches of all that they saw. Within a week, Perry learned later, these first pictures of the 'hairy barbarians' and their strange ships had been sold to the owners of print-shops, coloured, copied, carved on wood-blocks and began to appear on banners, screens, scrolls, fans and even towels throughout the city of Yedo [Edo].

Later that same day, large, flat-bottomed barges put out from Uraga and these carried local government officials, called *yakunin*, garbed in stiff ceremonial robes with high lacquered hats tied on their heads. There then ensued a parley between the Japanese and the foreigners carried out in the cumbersome order of English to Dutch to Japanese and back again which was to impede and complicate all these East-West communications for quite a time—until, in fact, sufficient linguists were trained so that the intermediary of Dutch could be dispensed with. During the discussion, Perry let it be known that he would not speak to anyone lower than the Governor of Uraga, that he had letters from his President to the ruler of Japan which he wished to deliver personally and that—this last in response to a plea from the barge below—that he had no intention of retreating south to Nagasaki and there was nothing the Japanese could do to make him.

A Pose of Dignity

The Commodore himself did not appear. He had adopted the pose of a secluded, omnipotent leader whose face men did not look upon lightly and whose cabin was soon entitled by the Japanese 'The Abode of the High and Mighty Mysteriousness'. Accustomed to such imperious behaviour from their own rulers, the Japanese were suitably impressed; they sent the Governor of Uraga himself to speak with the strangers. The Governor was, by American standards, a very short man and, clad in baggy golden trousers, wide-sleeved brocade jacket and shining lacquer clogs, he looked, commented Hawks, 'like an unusually brilliant knave of trumps'. Nevertheless, the Governor behaved with amiability, elegance and dignity on board the flagship and entered with zest into a discussion of plans for Perry's visit to the shore. Whilst drinking champagne with great composure, he also made it plain to the Americans that he knew quite well where they had come from and what their deck-guns were for.

And, indeed, while these preliminary contacts were being made, it became evident that the Shogun and his government were reacting speedily to the presence of these weapons so un-

expectedly and immovably trained on their innocent shore. Survey crews sent out from the *Susquehanna* reported that the coastline was a warren of anxious activity: women and children carried baskets of stones slung from a pole over their shoulders to
help strengthen the new earthworks; farmers turned grooms
brought their horses and carts to aid the soldiers in the anticipated battle; *samurai* and their retainers from far and wide refur-
bished their war-dresses, feathered their arrows, polished their
swords and hurried to the camps which were mushrooming on
the plain behind Uraga.

The Red Carpet

But when the news was confirmed that His High and Mighty
Mysteriousness would land to deliver the letters from the American President to his 'great and good friend' the ruler of Japan,
preparations of a more conciliatory nature began on shore. A
huge structure of wood and cloth was erected, the pyramid-

THE HARRIS TREATY OF 1858

*A year after his first visit, Commodore Perry returned to Japan and
concluded the Kanagawa friendship treaty of 1854. Four years later,
the United States sent Consul Townsend Harris to follow up with
a trade treaty. Article VI, keeping Americans free of Japanese courts,
caused particular resentment in Japan.*

The Treaty of Amity and Commerce Between the United
States and Japan, 1858

ARTICLE I. There shall henceforth be perpetual peace and
friendship between the United States of America and His
Majesty the Ty-Coon [i.e., *shōgun*] of Japan and his successors.

ARTICLE II. The President of the United States, at the re-
quest of the Japanese Government, will act as a friendly me-
diator in such matters of difference as may arise between the
Government of Japan and any European Power.

The ships-of-war of the United States shall render friendly

shaped roof of which looked from a distance, said Hawks, like three grain-ricks. A raised path was built from this to the jetty, and the jetty itself was bolstered with rocks and sacks of straw and sand. To make sure that the barbarians did not see too much, the camps of the soldiers and the outskirts of the village were sheltered behind high screens of rough cloth stretched between bamboo poles, the cloths emblazoned with the crests of all the clans present.

First there was a lull while the foreigners celebrated their Sunday—Bibles in every sailor's hand, a band on deck and the martial Christian strains of a hundred manly voices proclaiming that 'Before Jehovah's awful Throne, Ye nations, bow with sacred joy'. This scene, incidentally, which some might contemplate with misgiving nowadays, brought great satisfaction to a certain historian, Professor William Griffis, who arrived in Japan twenty years later and described it in his work *The Mikado's Empire*. He cites as an encouraging instance of the hymn's impact that 'Where cannon

---

aid and assistance to such Japanese vessels as they may meet on the high seas, so far as can be done without a breach of neutrality; and all American Consuls residing at ports visited by Japanese vessels shall also give them such friendly aid as may be permitted by the laws of the respective countries in which they reside.

ARTICLE III. In addition to the ports of Simoda [Shimoda] and Hakodade [Hokodate], the following ports and towns shall be opened on the dates respectively appended to them, that is to say: Kanagawa, on the 4th of July, 1859; Nagasaki, on the 4th of July, 1859; Nee-e-gata [Niigata], on the 1st of January, 1860; Hiogo [Hyogo], on the 1st of January, 1863. . . .

ARTICLE VI. Americans committing offenses against Japanese shall be tried in American Consular courts, and, when guilty, shall be punished according to American law. Japanese committing offenses against Americans shall be tried by the Japanese authorities and punished according to Japanese law.

David J. Lu, *Japan: A Documentary History.* Armonk, NY: M.E. Sharpe, Inc., 1997.

were cast to resist Perry, now stands the Imperial Females Normal College, an institution for young Christian converts.'

At last, on the fourteenth, the landing took place. American officers, marines and musicians from each ship, about three hundred in all, filled their small boats and headed shorewards, flags fluttering on every stern and a salute of guns behind them. To a certain Captain Buchanan fell the distinction of being the first westerner for over two hundred years to land in Japan with such uncompromising official pomp and, according to Griffis, the watching *samurai* growled in protest as Buchanan's foot crunched into the soil of their sacred country. With due decorum the whole western contingent formed into procession on the path leading to the Audience Hall: first two young ensigns carrying the box of letters; next Commodore Perry, martially erect even to the plume on his cocked hat; on either side of him, most amazing to Japanese eyes, an American Negro, 'two of the best-looking fellows of their colour that the squadron could furnish', Hawks recorded. Then came various officers, gilt buttons glinting in regular rows, epaulettes encrusted with gold stars; a few marines in correct, scarlet-slashed trousers and a band, its silver trumpets sounding, cymbals clashing, drums rolling. 'And all this parade', Hawks confesses, 'was but for effect.'

And then the foreigners, in their turn, saw strange sights.

Americans in Yokohama, Japan, during the 1850s.

Along the beach, on either side of the path, stood rank upon rank of Japanese soldiers, encased in ribbed armour of leather and iron, bright banners of emerald, royal-blue or orange flying high above their heads. Behind them solid lines of cavalry were drawn up, the riders' horned helmets spiking at the sky, their jewelled swords sheathed, but handy, and on their flanks standard-bearers whose crimson swallow-tailed pennons swept ten fluttering feet to the ground.

Meeting the Leaders

The foreigners marched upon the path to the Audience Hall. Here the body of the procession waited while the coloured striped cloths guarding the entrance were held apart for Perry and a small group of officers, and they were ushered inside. The interior was warm, quiet and shaded. The walls were soft with hangings of violet silk divided by heavy tasselled skeins of white, blue and rose. At the far end of the thick-matted chamber was a dais with a red felt covering, and on the dais, patient and still as china dolls, sat the official representatives of the Shogun's government in their padded, embroidered robes of ceremony. Perry and his men halted in silence. Then the westerners were motioned to sit in front of the dais—on chairs, incidentally, which had been hastily rounded up from the local temples, where they were normally used only by Buddhist priests during the conduct of a funeral service.

Finally the interpreters spoke. The box was delivered and the Commodore firmly explained its weighty contents: the President, he said, wanted peace with Japan and wanted to make a treaty so that trade could flourish across the Pacific between his great country and theirs, and then Japan too, would grow great and prosperous in her own right. Perry added that he would be back in the spring to receive the Japanese answer—bringing with him a larger squadron of ships. In twenty minutes it was all over. Blinking in the harsh sun outside the officers called their men to attention, the band clattered into action and the westerners returned safely to their black ships.

Friendly Encounters

During the rest of the squadron's stay there was some fraternisation. Survey crews went out continually trying to map a little of the coast and dubbing each landmark with a suitably impressive name—Perry Island, Mississippi Bay, Treaty Point and so on. Some sailors were allowed on shore, though a very tight rein was kept on their activities. Local officials visited every American ship bearing gifts of eggs, fowls and *saké* (rice wine), and received in return bottles of liquor, puddings and bags of potato and sweet-corn seed, for the Commodore had issued strict orders that no sailor was to leave an unpaid debt of any kind behind. Yezaimon, the Uraga Governor, who had shed his earlier fears and was enjoying himself greatly, bombarded his western hosts with questions—about their trains, their printing-machines, their navigational instruments and, above all, how it was that their ships could move so quickly against the wind. Captain Buchanan promised him that when they returned in the spring, the westerners would bring presents for the Emperor including a locomotive on rails and a wire which would stretch from Uraga to Yedo and through which you could speak from one place to another in a single second. Yezaimon, recorded Hawks, was helpless with envy.

Three days after the audience ashore, Perry decided that no more could be accomplished for the moment; he had to wait, impatiently, for the spring. So, early on the morning of 17 July, just nine days after their arrival, whistles blew, anchor-chains rattled, bells rang on board, sailors leaning over the rails exchanged good-byes with fishermen bobbing in the junks below and the black ships puffed steadily away over the horizon, against the wind. And Commodore Perry recorded with satisfaction in his journal that 'to a maritime people, the contrast between their weak junks and slight shallops and our powerful vessels must have made a deep impression'. And that was indeed the case. The Americans left behind not only a deep impression of impregnable strength and vastly superior technical skill, but, even worse, an awful threat, an incalculable promise: their return in the spring.

The Meiji Era

By Ki Kimura

The trade treaty with the United States, and the ones that followed with other nations, created a sense of humiliation and resentment among many Japanese, especially the once-proud samurai warriors. Rising discontent pushed the tottering Tokugawa dynasty over the edge. Throughout Japan the revolutionary cry went up: "Restore the Emperor, expel the Barbarian!" In 1868, the last of the shoguns abdicated, and the restoration took place. It opened one of the most remarkable eras in Japanese history: the reign of Emperor Meiji. Within twenty years, Japan had a modern industrial base, a powerful military, and a constitution that created, at least on paper, a parliamentary democracy. Japanese historian and novelist Ki Kimura describes how in the late nineteenth century his medieval nation made a great leap forward.

Early in 1868 a young man whom the world was to know as the Emperor Meiji [i.e., enlightened peace] emerged into history from behind the curtain of courtiers and ceremony that had for centuries isolated the Japanese throne.

For more than two hundred years Japan had remained a closed country, ruled by Shoguns (military governors) who had reduced the emperor to a figurehead. But by the middle of the nineteenth century this self-enforced isolation of Japan suddenly came to an end. Besieged by foreign powers clamoring for the country to open up to Western commerce, and threatened by rebellious feudal lords, the fifteenth Tokugawa Shogun yielded power to the Imperial house.

The youthful Meiji Emperor, Mitsuhito, and his dynamic advisers opened Japan not only to Western ideas and commerce but to all the tempestuous currents of the nineteenth century world. The Meiji Restoration . . . was like the bursting of a dam behind which had accumulated the energies and forces of centuries. Japan set out to achieve in only a few decades what had taken centuries to develop in the West: the creation of a modern nation, with modern industries and political institutions, and a modern pattern of society.

Top Hats and Tails

Young Samurai changed their Japanese dress for top hats and dark suits and sailed off to Europe and America to study Western techniques of government, industry—and war. In a tour de force of modernization, the Meiji revolutionaries raised their country to be a peer of the Western powers, in less than forty years—and without sacrificing Japan's traditional culture.

The events leading to the Restoration started the year after Meiji was born, when Commodore Matthew Perry's "black ships" from the United States steamed into Kurihama Bay in 1853 on a mission of diplomacy and commerce.

After Perry signed a treaty of amity with the Shogun the next spring, Russia, the Netherlands and Great Britain secured similar agreements. Hermit Japan, after secluding itself for over two hundred years, slowly began to resume contact with the outside world.

A Poor and Stagnant Nation

When Japan reopened its doors, it was stagnating under a feudal system which had divided society into four distinct castes: warriors, farmers, artisans and tradesmen. So all-pervasive was this caste system that it exercised control over the very lives of the people to the extent of prescribing exact rules on all activities relating to daily life and behavior. Even the use of language, both written and spoken was determined by the individual's social class.

The Confucian ethic, with its emphasis on the practice and cultivation of the cardinal virtues of filial piety, kindness, righteousness, propriety, intelligence, and faithfulness, constituted the foundation on which all relations between superiors and inferiors, one's obedience to authority, and the concept of master-servant were formalized. Society was stable, but totally immobilized.

The Japan of those days was moreover an impoverished agrarian state. Even in the late 1870s, some 75 to 80 percent of the employed population were engaged in agriculture. Per capita annual income was estimated at about $65. In other words, Japan was a nation sustained by a farming community working at a bare subsistence level.

Right from the time of Perry and the first treaties the Japanese were interested in international relations on the basis of independence and equality. There was a danger, they felt, that the Great Powers might dominate them, and a way of thinking, not in terms of the clan but in terms of the state, was born from this feeling.

The confrontation between groups advocating an open-door policy and those who urged the exclusion of foreigners was, for a time, bitter. Both factions had the same goal: to preserve national independence. When the champions of seclusion realized that this freedom could be maintained only through intercourse with foreigners, they made common cause with their former opponents.

Conflict also arose over whether Japan should return political power to the throne or continue the traditional Shogunate system of government. Again, national independence was the determining factor.

In 1867, both the Shogun and Emperor Komei, Meiji's father, died. The young Emperor and the new Shogun, Yoshinobu were duly installed in the highest offices of the land.

Yoshinobu was a man of vision, convinced that Japanese independence hinged on the country being unified and modernized. In late 1867, encouraged by a coalition of fiefs led by the strong provincial clans known as the "Satcho Dohi," he surrendered his authority to the Emperor and ended seven hundred years of military rule.

Sweeping Changes

In February 1868, the Reformation began: Emperor Meiji assumed supreme executive authority, and informed foreign representatives that his title should replace the Shogun's in all existing treaties.

Encouraged by his counselors, many of whom he chose from the Samurai, Japan's warrior class, Meiji broke the strict prohibition which barred foreigners from the capital, Kyoto, and received the representatives of the Great Powers in a New Year's audience. He also cast away the feudal edict against travel, and journeyed the twenty-seven miles from Kyoto to Osaka to attend a naval review.

His major step in the first year of the Reformation came when he summoned his nobles to the royal palace and, in their presence, took the "charter oath" by which he promised that a deliberative assembly would be formed, all classes would share in the government, and that justice, not ancient custom, would in future be the guiding principle of the administration.

In the same year, he separated Japan further from its past by moving the capital from Kyoto to Edo and renaming it Tokyo, or Eastern Capital.

In the beginning, the Reformation's leaders devoted almost all their energies to developing a sound economic base for the new state: the monetary system had to be stabilized, taxes levied, new industry developed, and foreign markets opened.

One prerequisite change was the abolition of the feudal system which, with autocratic chieftains governing and levying taxes over huge estates, stood squarely in the way of economic

THE UNEQUAL TREATIES

Following the pattern set by the Harris Treaty, Western powers forced Japan to accept unequal treaty terms. Historian Louis Perez describes the features that Japan found particularly humiliating.

The unequal treaties were international conventions signed by Japan between the years 1854 and 1873 that granted extraterritorial privileges and fixed conventional tariffs to sixteen Western nations. The treaties contained eight distinctive characteristics that set them apart from those conventions between Western states.

First, they were unilateral, not reciprocal. That is, they granted rights and privileges to foreigners in Japan, but not to Japanese who were abroad. Second, two cities and five ports (collectively known as "Treaty Ports") in Japan were open for trade and residence to foreigners. Third, the foreigners in these ports and cities lived apart from the Japanese in "settlements" and in some cases were allowed to legislate and administer regulations within these communities.

Fourth, diplomatic officers were the only aliens allowed free and unlimited access into the interior of Japan. Fifth, the treaties contained no expiration date and made no real provision for their termination either unilaterally or by mutual consent. Sixth, customs duties which were controlled jointly by Japanese and Westerners, were fixed at

progress. No central government could effectively unify Japan if it continued to exist. Feudalism had been a way of life since the twelfth century, and the clans were strong. Yet such was the spirit of the times that the four great Satcho Dohi clans of the west returned their estates to the Emperor in 1869, and entreated him to reorganize them under a uniform set of laws. The lesser clans soon followed, and between 1871 and 1872 the four classes of warrior, artisan, farmer and tradesman were abolished.

The most important factor in Japan's economic development

an artificially low 5% ad valorem. Seventh, a most favored nation clause stipulated that any and all concessions granted by the Japanese to any nation were automatically granted to all treaty powers. Eighth, all citizens of the treaty nations enjoyed extraterritorial privileges that rendered them, for all intents and purposes, immune from Japanese justice.

As far as the Japanese were concerned, the two most onerous and humiliating aspects of the treaties were the provisions granting extraterritoriality and fixing the tariff. The tariff created many difficulties in Japan because the nation was deprived of more than half of the revenue that Western nations routinely collected in customs. Not only were the rates artificially low in 1866 when they had been set, but no periodic adjustments were allowed, so that twenty years later, fiscal inflation made them closer to 3%. Japan was forced to depend most heavily on land tax revenue, which acted as a drain on the economy and caused inflation. As burdensome as the fixed tariff was, the damage incurred by extraterritoriality, or more properly, consular jurisdiction, was much more treacherous and insidious. Not only did consular jurisdiction deprive Japan of its judicial sovereignty, but it also imposed a deep sense of shame on the Japanese, because it implied that their society and culture were inferior to those of the West.

Louis G. Perez, *Japan Comes of Age: Mutsu Munemitsu and the Revision of the Unequal Treaties.* Cranbury, NJ: Associated University Presses, 1999.

was a strong and integrated control by the central government. This strength was needed to enforce three difficult decisions made in the first half of Meiji's reign, and which were to have enduring effects on Japan's prosperity.

First, the government resisted the temptation to unite the country through foreign military adventures. Six years after the young Emperor took power, strong members of the government favored going to war with Korea after Korean shore batteries had fired on a Japanese gunboat. Despite the fact that such action would have temporarily unified the country, which was plagued by discontented elements at the time, the proposal was rejected in 1873, and the nation's energies were turned to solving domestic problems.

The second decision was to deflate the economy in 1881. Serious inflation at that time made it difficult to promote modern industry and investment. Disregarding public dissatisfaction, the Meiji government firmly introduced stringent fiscal measures that halted inflation in 1884, with the result that the economic goals set in 1868 were achieved in 1885, as planned.

The third decision concerned the financing of new industry. The Meiji leaders avoided the comparatively easy solution of allowing foreign investment, reasoning that it might make Japan dependent on foreign nations. Instead, they raised the necessary funds by instituting a land tax. Investment from abroad was restricted.

Promoting Industry

Meiji Japan built its modern industry on a traditional foundation. Raw silk and tea were the original mainstays of Japan's exports, and these were encouraged (even the Empress set up a cocoonery in the palace grounds to promote sericulture) because their foreign exchange earning power helped establish new industries.

Hokkaido, then a vast virgin island at the north of the Japanese archipelago, was opened up with American assistance. Agriculture and Japan's chemical industry (today the second in the world) were started. Apple trees, never before seen in Japan, were planted, and the first dairy industry was begun.

After seeing its success in the West, the Meiji leaders believed firmly in private enterprise. But centuries of feudalism had left the country with few industrial traditions or skills, and Japanese investors were cautious about risking their capital in new and sometimes strange ventures.

To foster industrial growth, joint-stock companies were encouraged, with emphasis on foreign-exchange firms, trading companies and transportation companies; government subsidies were granted to key businesses and industries, and favorable tax concessions made.

The government also built model factories in the steel, cement, plate glass, firebrick, woolen textiles and spinning industries. They were set up on a profit-making basis but with the primary aim of introducing European production methods and techniques into Japan.

In all its efforts to modernize industry, the Reformation leaders were aided and encouraged by Emperor Meiji who traveled throughout the islands, inspecting shipyards, opening factories, and visiting development areas.

Reforms in other fields were far reaching: education was made compulsory, all restrictions were lifted on Japanese going abroad, Christianity was permitted, vaccinations, postal service, telegraphs, and steamships were introduced, torture was abolished, European dress was prescribed for officials (with the Emperor showing the way by adopting Western military dress), and European and American advisers were freely employed.

An Educational Push

Great efforts were made in the field of education; the government knew that for Japan to be wealthy and strong, the intellectual level of the people had to be raised. The Japanese appetite for knowledge had already been whetted under the Tokugawa Shoguns when private temple schools flourished, and the study of Western science, primarily in the medical field, was pursued through Nagasaki, the only city open to foreign trade.

Before the Reformation, education had progressed to the point where 50 percent of the male population and 15 percent of the female population had received some formal instruction.

A policy of equal opportunity was established in Meiji Japan. To draw gifted students from poor homes, education was made free at military academies and teacher-training schools and colleges. . . .

In 1890, the Emperor ordered that "the guiding principles of school education be compiled in an "Imperial Rescript on Education." It enjoined all students to honor their ancestors, respect their parents, be loyal to superiors and serve their country.

That the educational policy was successful can be seen from

the fact that by 1885, 42 percent of the students at Tokyo Imperial University were commoners compared to 25 percent in 1878, and at the end of the Meiji era, primary school attendance was 95 percent.

This love of learning of the Japanese people, coupled with an academic level which was extremely advanced, although limited to a narrow sphere, provided the conditions necessary, once Western instruction was introduced, to bring about an amazing dissemination of general education, and produced scholars of international caliber. . . .

Liberal Critics

Japan's modernization was carried out to counter the impact of the West, and the much needed reforms were mainly instituted by the strong central government. Yet, those outside the government, including its critics, also worked collectively for Japan's renewal.

For example, Yukichi Fukuzawa, a pioneer educator, in expressing his opposition to the tendency toward an increasing governmental predominance, established Japan's first private institution of higher learning, Keio University. Nevertheless, he was always concerned with the independence of the state and, as an educator, he worked for its betterment by increasing the capabilities of his fellow Japanese.

Emori Ueki, a prominent liberal politician, was another example of "creative opposition." While severely criticizing the authoritarian Meiji government by preaching freedom and equality, he declared that any person who did not extend his capacities and utilize his talents was failing the nation.

Taisuke Itagaki, another liberal of the Reformation, was tireless in his efforts to persuade the government to institute a deliberative assembly, and in 1881 it issued an edict declaring that a national parliament would be established in 1890 with the intervening nine years to be devoted to government preparations for an orderly change.

Hirobumi Ito, one of the statesmen who played a major role in reshaping Japan, was sent to Europe in the same year to study Western governments, and determine which one should serve as the model for Japan. After evaluating the American, British, and French systems, he chose the Imperial German constitution as best suited for Japan's needs. It provided for an elected assembly, but made the government responsible to the throne. In 1889, Emperor Meiji promulgated the new constitution, and one year later the legislature was convened.

Treaty Battles

Parallel to governmental, social and industrial progress, the Japanese took on the considerable task of persuading their foreign treaty partners to revise the terms of their agreements. The existing treaties, which favored the foreign signatories with low import duties (mostly·5 percent), and gave their citizens exemption from Japanese law courts, had been signed under vastly different conditions.

It took eleven years for Japan to get the terms it wanted. The break came when Great Britain finally agreed to a new treaty abolishing extraterritoriality, and giving Japan the right to set its own import tariffs. Similar treaties with other countries were soon concluded, and the Emperor fixed 1899 as the year that they would come into force.

During this time, foreign wars had been avoided, but in 1894–1895, Japan declared war on China over Korea and defeated the Chinese on the battlefield. In 1904 hostilities broke out with Russia, Japanese troops entering Manchuria. A peace treaty was signed the following year.

During the remainder of Emperor Meiji's reign, Japan moved within the circle of great powers consolidating its position as a vital component of international politics and trade.

On July 30, 1912, Emperor Meiji died at the age of fifty-nine. Under him, Japan had emerged from behind the ritual screen that had shielded it from the rest of the world to become the leading power in Asia and a peer of the West.

The revolution that Meiji presided over was even more remarkable in that it was orderly and controlled, and enhanced the monarchy rather than destroyed it, a result mainly due to the capable leaders who, in this period of "Enlightened Rule," shaped the new Japan.

Battling for Control in Asia

By W.G. Beasley

With Japan's swift industrialization following the 1868 Restoration, the Meiji government became increasingly anxious to secure access to raw materials in Asia. At least as important was the quest for status. Only by becoming a colonial power, Japanese leaders believed, could their country gain recognition as an equal from the West. The Japanese military eagerly sought opportunities for foreign conquest. Japan skirmished with China over Taiwan in 1873 and sent a naval expedition to force a treaty on Korea in 1875. Less than twenty years later, Japan launched a series of wars on the Asian continent that was to culminate in an astonishing victory over Russia for dominance of northern China and colonization of Korea. University of London historian W.G. Beasley explains how by 1915 Japan emerged as the most powerful nation in Asia.

I n June 1894 a number of local revolts broke out in Korea, organized by anti-Western, traditionalist groups called Tong-haks. The king, acknowledging his tribute status, called on China for help in suppressing them. This was quickly sent. Japan, however, held that the action was contrary to the Tientsin convention of 1885. She therefore sent forces to maintain her own position, shifting the focus from the Tong-hak outbreaks to the much more dangerous issue of Sino-Japanese rivalry.

There were several specific reasons why the Japanese government was not inclined on this occasion to act with restraint. Its army, led by Yamagata Aritomo, had come to view Korea as potentially an element in Japan's defences, not least because Russia had started to build a railway to her own possessions in the north. Political parties in the Diet, urged on by patriot-activists and a volatile public, claimed that national honour was at stake, making caution difficult. More soberly, the Prime Minister, Ito Hirobumi, and the Foreign Minister, Mutsu Munemitsu, saw a prospect of political and economic gains, sufficient to make the international risks arising from war with China seem worthwhile. Hence Ito set out to force a confrontation. At the end of June 1894, far from withdrawing Japanese troops, as China demanded, he announced his intention of keeping them in the peninsula until the Korean government had carried out an extensive catalogue of reforms, the main thrust of which would be to substitute Japanese for Chinese influence. In July he warned China to send in no more men. Shortly afterwards his own took over the Korean royal palace. Since China's government, too, was under domestic pressures, there was from this point no hope of avoiding war. Its formal declaration came at the beginning of August.

Swift Victory

By the end of September 1894—to the surprise not only of China, but also of the world—the Japanese army controlled most of Korea, while the navy had command of the Yellow Sea. In October two divisions under Yamagata crossed into southern Manchuria. Three more under Oyama Iwao moved against the Liaotung peninsula, capturing Port Arthur the following month. Occupation of Weihaiwei in February 1895 then gave Japan outposts on both sides of the sea approaches to Peking, forcing China to come to terms. Li Hung-chang was sent to negotiate them with Ito Hirobumi at Shimonoseki.

Japanese ambitions had grown with the tale of victories until they exceeded by far the original aim of prising Korea loose from Chinese tutelage. As presented to Li Hung-chang early in 1895 they included demands for an indemnity; for the handing over to Japan of Taiwan (which she had not even occupied) and Liaotung; and for a commercial treaty, which would put Japanese privileges in China on a par with those of the Western powers. In addition, Weihaiwei was to be held by Japan until the indemnity was paid. Li Hung-chang had little choice but to accede, with the result that a peace treaty on these lines was signed in April.

To the Japanese people the fruits of victory seemed very sweet. Their government, however, knew them to be at risk, for they were subject to the concurrence of the powers. It was partly for this reason that the proposed commercial arrangements were to include several benefits, long sought by foreign merchants, which all the powers could share through the operation of the

most-favoured-nation clause. However, no such benefit attached
to the cession of Liaotung. Japan maintained that the peninsula
was needed for the defence of Korea. Russia, on the other hand,
saw it as a threat to her own route to China through Manchuria.
Accordingly, on 23 April 1895 the Russian representative in
Tokyo, supported by those of France and Germany, informed
Mutsu Munemitsu that his government viewed with concern the
prospect of Liaotung being transferred to Japan, since this would
menace Peking and hence the peace of Asia. Japan was 'advised'
to return the territory to China. Knowing that Russia, at least,
seemed willing to back the demand with force, whereas there was
little prospect of help from Britain or America, the Ito cabinet
submitted (5 May). All Japan could get to salve her pride was an
increase in the size of the indemnity.

A Painful Reversal

Pride, there is no doubt, was at the heart of the matter, as seen
from Tokyo. The loss of the clause concerning Liaotung did not
by any means rob the treaty of its value, but the manner of the
loss affected Japanese opinion as if it had. The war had brought
a tremendous wave of enthusiasm at home, silencing even the
government's critics in the Diet. Victory had been hailed with
exultation. Then came a savage reminder that half a century's
work had still not put Japan in a position to ignore or reject the
'advice' of one of the major powers. It is no wonder that the
shock was great and that it engendered a mood of bitterness. . . .

Japan was left with only economic opportunities, which she
had to deal directly with Russia to confirm, though the Nishi-
Rosen agreement of April 1898, by which both sides undertook
to refrain from interference in Korean politics and to consult each
other before sending military or financial advisers there, gave her
some reassurance on that score.

Of more general importance for Japan were the changes
which were taking place in China at this time. China's defeat in
1894–5 had led some of the powers to doubt the continued vi-
ability of the treaty port system and to consider other ways of in-
suring their interests. In the first place, those who had 'saved'
China from Japan after Shimonoseki called in their debts by
claiming spheres of influence in various parts of the country, that
is, exclusive railway and mining rights in designated areas, each
defended by a small leased territory and a naval base. France

carved out such a sphere in the southern provinces, bordering Indo-China, and Germany in Shantung. Russia followed suit in Manchuria, where she took over Port Arthur in Liaotung—only recently denied at her instance to Japan—which was to be linked by rail to the Russian-owned Chinese Eastern Railway, already under construction between Baikal and Vladivostock.

Turmoil in China

These developments took place between 1896 and 1898. Britain and the United States viewed them with disapproval, but made no immediate attempt to stop what was going on. Japan, who also disapproved, was too weak to do anything on her own; and rejection of her approach to China, designed to pick up privileges in Fukien, opposite Taiwan, demonstrated that she lacked the means to compete in this kind of company. Her attention was in any case soon distracted by events in the north. In 1899 and 1900 a series of anti-foreign outbreaks, led by groups called Boxers, swept through China's northern provinces. The Peking legations of the powers came under siege, and in the next few months Japan won international reputation by providing the bulk of the troops for the expedition that relieved them. However, she found herself immediately afterwards faced by a more considerable challenge, especially to her position in Korea, when Russia seized most of Manchuria on the pretext that Boxers threatened the railway installations there.

Out of all this turbulence came a realignment of the powers. France and Germany continued to support Russia as they had done in 1895, though not wholeheartedly. Britain and America came together in what was called the policy of the Open Door, aimed at preserving equality of opportunity for foreign trade in China. This left Japan to make a choice between the rival groups, since she could not stand alone. She did not find it easy. On the one hand, free competition in the China trade was not altogether to her taste, because her industry had not yet reached a level at which it could challenge those of Britain and America on equal terms. On the other, co-operation with Russia was only likely to be possible at the cost of accepting Russian domination of the mainland north of the Great Wall. To put it differently, the choice was between extending trade with China's central and southern provinces under Britain's auspices, or securing a greater stake in Korea as the price of a deal with Russia. The dilemma was in one form or another to be central to Japanese policy decisions for the next thirty years.

The first occasion for debating it arose from proposals for an alliance with Britain in the summer of 1901. There had already been private overtures which suggested that such an arrangement might be feasible, on the grounds that both countries had an interest in opposing any further Russian advance. For Britain, the question still to be decided was whether Japanese help would make it worth abandoning 'splendid isolation'. For Japan, it was what Russia might be induced to concede by way of alternative. Ito Hirobumi preferred to wait until there had been an approach to St Petersburg to see what was on offer, but the Prime Minister, Katsura Taro, and his patron, Yamagata Aritomo, both believed that a show-down with Russia would be inevitable before very long, which made them reluctant to spend any effort to avoid it. Consequently, Ito was by-passed; the negotiations with Britain were pressed forward; and a treaty of alliance was signed on 30 January 1902, providing that each signatory would remain neutral if the other became involved in a Far East war, except that they would act together if either were attacked by two powers or more. This meant that Britain would hold the ring against any possible renewal of the Triple Intervention. In addition, Britain recognized that Japan possessed interests in Korea 'in a peculiar degree politically as well as commercially and industrially'.

Prelude to War

In April 1902, apparently in response to this pressure, Russia agreed to withdraw her forces from Manchuria by six-month stages. However, the second stage of withdrawal, due in April 1903, was delayed without explanation. The Japanese government therefore decided to seek a more general settlement with Russia, now that it could be done from a position of greater strength, taking as its basis what her Foreign Minister, Komura Jutaro, called *Man-Kan kōkan*, 'exchanging Manchuria for Korea'. He envisaged, that is, an undertaking by both countries to respect the territorial integrity of China and Korea, coupled with recognition of Russian railway rights in Manchuria and of Japan's much broader interests in Korea. Russia's counter-claim (October 1903) sought more for Russia in Manchuria, less for Japan in Korea. These terms Komura, in the light of an increasingly aggressive public opinion at home, could not possibly entertain. He restated his demands in the form of an ultimatum (January 1904), which was clearly a prelude to war.

War was declared on 10 February, but hostilities had already begun two days earlier. There was fighting at first in Korea and along the coast towards Liaotung. In April a naval victory outside Port Arthur gave Japan control of the seas across which she needed to move her reinforcements, thereby enabling her First Army to strike north across the Yalu River into Manchuria in May and her Second Army to land in the Liaotung peninsula a few days later. Within a month General Nogi Maresuke's Third Army had laid siege to Port Arthur itself. There followed nearly a year of campaigning: a battle round Liaoyang in August and early September 1904; the capture of Port Arthur at the beginning of January 1905; then an advance against Mukden in February and March, involving no less than sixteen Japanese divisions. As a final blow to Russian hopes, the Russian Baltic fleet, which had sailed halfway round the world to break the blockade of Vladivostock, was met by Admiral Togo Heihachiro's forces in the Tsushima Straits in May and decisively defeated.

Russia Cedes Territory

Both sides had by then good reasons to end the struggle. Russia was facing revolution at home. Japan was unable any longer to sustain casualties and expenditure at existing levels. Accordingly, when America offered mediation, a truce was agreed, then a peace conference at Portsmouth, New Hampshire, held in August 1905. Japan's representative was Komura. His overriding objective had long been to secure for his country a position from which she could defend her mainland interests without outside help, should the rivalries of the powers bring China to collapse. Spelling this out, he had written in July 1904 that Korea 'must be brought effectively within the sphere of our sovereignty'; Manchuria 'must be made in some degree a sphere of interest'; and there should be an extension of Japan's economic privileges to the Russian territories in the north. Despite Japan's weakness at the end of the war, much of this survived the peace negotiations. Japan gained Russian recognition of her freedom of action in Korea, and took over the Russian lease of Liaotung (Kwantung), plus that part of the railway which linked it with Harbin (renamed the South Manchuria Railway). She also secured the cession from Russia of the southern half of Sakhalin

(Karafuto). There was no indemnity, but Komura had good cause to be pleased with the Treaty of Portsmouth, which he signed on 5 September 1905. It did not satisfy the extravagant expectations of the Japanese public, however. News of it caused riots in Tokyo, bringing martial law to the capital for a day or two. . . .

Victory for Ito and his allies did not mean that the disagreement came to an end. In the years that followed, while the Foreign Ministry became spokesman for the Ito–Inoue line, looking to financial circles for support, the army—notably the Kwantung Army, which had been established in the leased territory of Liaotung—took every opportunity to assert its independence in this matter. One consequence was that Japan moved towards treating the Manchurian question as something apart, falling outside the policy of the Open Door. Another was a local rapprochement with Russia. In July 1910 the two countries concluded a secret agreement laying down a division of spheres in Manchuria, Russia in the north, Japan in the south, which implied a willingness to co-operate in the face of any attempts by other powers to enforce the Open Door there.

Domination of Korea

There were no such difficulties about framing policy towards Korea, on which the Japanese were broadly agreed among themselves and had no reason to fear intervention from outside. During the war years Japan had used her status as an 'ally' to secure a position of dominance in Korea. In November 1905, having had indications that neither Britain nor the United States would raise objections, she negotiated a treaty of protectorate, appointing Ito as Resident-General in Seoul. This made it possible to obtain privileges by way of railway, mining, and fishery rights, plus timber concessions and land for Japanese residents. However, it did not stifle Korean opposition. In June 1907 the Korean ruler sent envoys secretly to the Hague to seek an international declaration of Korea's independence. They failed. Japan used the incident as a pretext to force the Korean emperor's abdication and to strengthen the hold of Japanese nominees on government. Most of the Korean army was thereupon disbanded.

After this, anti-Japanese dissidents in Korea turned to violence. Against a background of rising turbulence, the Japanese cabinet—Katsura was again Prime Minister—finally decided in the spring of 1909 that indirect control, such as was given by a protectorate, was not enough for its needs. It was resolved to move to outright annexation; the War Minister, Terauchi Masatake, was sent to Seoul as Resident-General (Ito had been assassinated by a Korean patriot in Harbin in October); and the Japanese garrison was strengthened. On 22 August 1910, once all preparations were complete, Terauchi signed a treaty of annexation which had been forced on the Korean court. He was then made Japan's first Governor-General of the colony.

Stymied in China

During these years Japan had been building a considerable economic stake in China, acting in concert with the other treaty powers. Like them, therefore, she had a good deal at risk when Chinese unrest at last became anti-Manchu revolution in the winter of 1911–12. The immediate outcome of the outbreak was confusion. It was some months before it was clear that there would be an end to Manchu rule, another year or more before Yuan Shih-k'ai, backed by much of the pre-revolutionary bureaucracy, overcame Sun Yat-sen in a contest for power. Japanese policy-makers found it difficult to decide how best to promote Japan's interests in this situation. The army sponsored two semi-official—and unsuccessful—attempts to organize an independent Manchuria under a Manchu figurehead. The Kokuryukai and its sympathizers gave their backing to Sun Yat-sen, providing arms for his followers with the help of Mitsui and other firms, which hoped to be given business advantages. Cabinets, by contrast, tended to follow the lead of the West in opting for Yuan Shih-k'ai, because he seemed more likely than any other Chinese to establish a state of order in which trade could flourish again; but they did not do so with enough conviction to persuade him that Japan could be counted as a friend. The result of these diverse interventions was that Yuan's victory over Sun in 1913 left Tokyo with little to show for nearly two years of meddling.

Despite this, all the Japanese groups which had been involved—government, army, businessmen, patriots—shared a conviction that Japan must seek a relationship with the new republican China that was closer and more clearly bilateral than that which the treaty port system had made possible so far.

A fresh opportunity to develop it came with the outbreak of war in Europe in August 1914. The terms of the Anglo-Japanese alliance did not require Japan to join the hostilities against Germany, but the Okuma cabinet decided that there was much to be gained by being a belligerent. It therefore demanded that Germany withdraw or disarm her warships in Far Eastern waters and surrender the leased territory which she held in Shantung. When the ultimatum was ignored, Japan declared war, landed troops in Shantung and seized the German bases there. In addition, naval operations, begun during October, brought the occupation of all German-held Pacific islands north of the equator.

Once these moves had been completed, the way was open to settle some of the outstanding issues in Japan's relations with China. As Foreign Minister, Kato Takaaki had inherited several items of unfinished business. In Manchuria Japan had for some time been trying to secure additional railway rights and to extend the duration of the leases taken over from Russia in 1905. Further south there was the question of the Hanyehping coal and iron company, which it was reported that Yuan Shih-k'ai was planning to nationalize. Since it was a major supplier to Japan's Yawata plant and heavily in debt to Japanese banks, significant economic interests were at stake. The disposal of German railway and mining rights in Shantung, which had now become an object of Japanese ambitions, was another matter to be decided. In a wider perspective, the army wanted to appoint military advisers to the Chinese government, for the sake of the influence this would give in matters of defence, and the Kokuryukai, in a document which Uchida Ryohei put forward in November, spoke of something more like a Japanese protectorate over China as a whole.

Renewed Pressure on China

Late in 1914 these various pieces were put together by the Foreign Ministry to form what became known as the Twenty-one Demands. In addition to the specific items concerned with Manchuria, Shantung, and Hanyehping, they included a clause requiring Peking 'not to cede or lease to any other power any harbour or bay or any island along the coast of China', while a final section (Group V), which was to provoke the greatest controversy, called for railway concessions in the lower Yangtse valley, prior consultation with Japan about any proposed foreign loan for the development of transport in the province of Fukien, the employment of 'influential Japanese' as political, financial, and military advisers in China, and priority for Japanese firms in the provision of China's military equipment. Even allowing for the fact that the points cited in Group V were described as 'highly desirable', not 'absolutely essential' like the rest, it was impossible to conceive of such gains being conceded without straining the fabric of the treaty port system.

The demands were presented privately to Yuan Shih-k'ai in January 1915, together with an offer of personal and political inducements for accepting them. Yuan appealed in vain for help to Britain and the United States. Once it was clear that this would not be forthcoming, Kato pressed his advantage home, dropping Group V, but making everything else the subject of an ultimatum. Treaties were signed on 25 May, accompanied by an exchange of supplementary notes, which together gave Japan everything her government, if not the Army and the patriots, sought.

The Emergence of Women

By Janet E. Hunter

For most of its recorded history, Japan has kept women firmly in sub-servient roles. In fact, says historian Janet E. Hunter, the position of women actually got worse in the centuries after the Kamakura period (starting around A.D. 1100). By the late Tokugawa period, she explains, Japanese women's primary duties were to give birth, raise children, and offer care and entertainment to men. As Japan modernized, however, economic changes led many women to work outside the home, often under miserable factory conditions, and that, in turn, gave rise to a women's rights movement. In this selection, Hunter portrays the changing conditions of women following the reopening of Japan.

The new exposure to Western civilization raised questions over the role and status of Japanese women. The years after the 1850s produced no immediate or dramatic change, but some women became active in spheres denied to them during the Tokugawa period and Western cultural influences began to stimulate a greater awareness of the position of women among the more educated. The first perceptible changes were essentially superficial. The initial craze for Western cultural habits was pursued by many female members of the ruling élite. Like men they adopted Western clothes and hairstyles; they were encouraged to participate in Western-style social gatherings to indicate to foreigners how Westernized Japan had become. . . .

Some of the earliest female activists were those who were in-fluenced by Christianity to campaign against concubinage and the existence of licensed prostitution in Japan. The Women's Temperance Association prominent in this activity was the Japan-ese counterpart of Western organizations such as the Women's Christian Temperance Union. The campaign was unsuccessful;

both licensed and unlicensed prostitution continued to be legal under national law until after World War II. Nevertheless it signified a limited advance towards a concept of women's rights, albeit within the confines of home and motherhood.

More radical women campaigned as part of the popular rights movement during the 1880s. Two of the best known of these were Kishida Toshiko (1864–1901) and Fukuda Hideko (1865–1927). Kishida, a former lady-in-waiting at court, was a source of inspiration to many women through her fiery speeches in support of women's being equal partners in the building of a new Japan. The outspokenness of her criticism of existing mores made her the subject of intimidation and harassment. Among those enthused by her oratory was Kageyama (later Fukuda) Hideko. Fukuda's association with the radical wing of the popular rights movement led to her imprisonment in 1885–9, but she remained a stalwart and vocal supporter of women's rights in the face of government suppression of the nascent socialist movement and acute poverty. She was dedicated to improving education opportunities and the chance of self-sufficiency for poorer women normally unable to afford them. Many of her later efforts were devoted to raising women's consciousness, particularly through journalistic activity. Though remaining doyenne of the women's movement until her death, Fukuda was an isolated figure. The decline of the popular rights movement put a severe damper on the women's rights' activity it had begun to stimulate. Kishida's activities became less public after her marriage in 1885, and with Fukuda in prison others, too, fell silent.

Economic Changes

Notwithstanding the ferment of 1882–5, the mass of women remained relatively untouched by the campaigns of Christians and popular rights activists. Far more significant for them were the changes wrought by the economic transformation taking place in the country, which forced more and more women to adopt a lifestyle at odds with the role and status traditionally ascribed to them. As the number of women employed outside the home grew rapidly from the early Meiji period, the role and occupations of women in the labour force changed dramatically. Women from the artisan and commercial classes had long engaged in business; their numbers now increased, although some existing handicraft industries and commercial undertakings were displaced by newer rivals. Millions of women continued to engage in the arduous, exhausting manual labour of farmwork. The nature of agricultural work altered little at this time; substantial increases in output and productivity were secured by more, rather than less, labour. Many peasant women had traditionally carried on occupations such as weaving and spinning within the home, but the growth of factory-based industry also drove an increasing number to work as wage labour outside the home for extended periods. The textile industries, the cornerstone of early industrialization, had a largely female workforce; around 250,000 women worked in factories by the turn of the century. Most were under twenty; temporary migrants *(dekasegi)* from farming villages, they remitted much of their wages to their families and worked at the most for a few years before returning to their communities to marry. Other women became secretaries, telephonists, teachers, nurses, clerks—a few at first, but from the 1890s in rapidly growing numbers. As women were increasingly able to choose whether to sell their labour to the agricultural or industrial sectors, the prospects and expectations of those employed in the new growth areas had a growing effect on those working outside them.

No Improvement

Economic as well as social change was thus driving women away from the roles which they had traditionally occupied. Yet the essential nature of women's work did not lead to improvements in status or rights. From the 1890s the establishment increasingly sought to reimpose traditional virtues and status on women. Given the difficulty of doing so in the face of dramatic economic and political changes, its success was substantial and long-lasting. Thirty to forty years after the Restoration the majority of Japanese, both men and women, still adhered closely to the Tokugawa ideal of a woman's role, and the new orthodoxy tried to build on and reinforce conservative attitudes of this kind.

The keystone of the political system, the Meiji Constitution of 1889, excluded women from any direct political participation, and other legislation prevented them from campaigning for change. Women began to agitate for the vote in the years after World War I, but legal hindrances rendered their activity constantly vulnerable to official intervention. A more pervasive restriction was embodied in the 1898 civil code, which became the legal foundation of the patriarchal family (*ie*) system in the pre-1945 period, and placed a woman firmly within the locus of the family. Every clause of the civil code relating to women reinforced their subordinate, subservient position in Japanese society. A woman had no independent legal status, but was treated as a minor; all legal agreements on her behalf were concluded by the male to whom she was subordinate—father, husband or son. She had no free choice of spouse or domicile. While women could, in theory, protest against this subordinate position in a non-political manner, to do so directly posed a challenge to the whole social orthodoxy on which the prewar Japanese state was founded. Women thus protested at their peril. Those who demonstrated their dissatisfaction by adopting non-conformist lifestyles or extra-marital sexual relationships could lay themselves open not merely to social opprobrium but to legal action.

Such women's organizations as existed in the late nineteenth century confined themselves to activities which met with official approval. The Christian Temperance movement concerned itself with temperance, prostitution and poverty. The Patriotic Women's Association of 1901 sought to provide physical and material comfort to soldiers and bereaved families in time of war. Upper class women were conspicuous in both these organizations, and although the Patriotic Women's Association, which had one million members by the end of World War I, could claim mass membership, activity at local level was minimal. Organizations such as the Patriotic Women's Association were essentially the creatures of the establishment.

Literature as Dissent

Significantly, literature remained a vehicle for dissent for both sexes, and in the case of women served as the genesis of a renewed political movement for women's rights. Literary expressions of defiance from women unable to develop their creative abilities or express themselves to the full grew into a broader resentment against the subordinate status of women and their lowly position in the 'family state'. This new direction was marked by the formation of the famous Bluestocking Society *(Seitōsha)* of 1911 by a small number of women graduates led by Hiratsuka Raichō (1886–1971). Strongly influenced by the romantic literary movement and the pacifist poet Yosano Akiko and other women writers, the group determined to secure for itself personal liberation through expression in its own journal. *Bluestocking (Seitō)* was the first Japanese journal to be edited and written by women. Hiratsuka's declaration in the first issue was a harbinger of later developments. Entitled 'Originally woman was the sun', the statement called on women to regain their 'hidden sun' and reject their position of dependence, in which they could only shine in the reflected light of their men. The implied criticism of the whole family system and existing pattern of male-female relationships alienated many critics from the start.

In successive issues *Bluestocking* found itself moving away from an exclusive concern with individual liberation to the problems of women in society as a whole. Persecution of the group increased. Hiratsuka herself was propelled by her search for personal liberation toward more anti-establishment views, and the struggle to keep the journal going in the face of growing censorship gradually eroded support. The editorship was handed over to the politically radical Itō Noe early in 1915, but her advocacy of anarchism weakened support for the journal still further. It ceased publication in 1916. The membership of the group was never great, nor the circulation of the journal ever more than a few thousand, but its influence was out of all proportion to its size. Hiratsuka herself remained a leader of the women's movement until her death. Many other leaders of the interwar and post-1945 women's movement were readers of the journal or members of the group, and many more were caught up in the renewed concern for the position of women in Japanese society which the Bluestockings had initiated. They included Ichikawa Fusae (1893–1981), one of the founders of the New Women's Association *(Shinfujin kyōkai)* of 1919, which campaigned for greater legal rights for women, and better education and welfare facilities for them. This organization and its successor, the Women's Suffrage League of 1925, pressed for an end to the legal prohibition of political activity by women and female suffrage. In 1922 a partial amendment of the 1900 Peace Police Law allowed women to attend and hold political meetings, but the right to join parties and to vote was withheld until after 1945.

Abuse of Women Workers

The Bluestockings and other intellectual groups searching for personal freedom were only one facet of women's rights activity after the Meiji period. Just as the 1880s popular rights movement had stimulated feminist ideas, so, too, did the emerging labour and socialist movements attract women who, despite their exclusion from political activity, sought to reassess the position of women in the light of socialist ideology and the growth of capitalist industry in Japan. The female industrial labour force grew rapidly after 1900, but although strikes by female workers in the 1880s had proved relatively successful, employers proved increasingly able to stifle sporadic communal expressions of protest. The majority of female workers endured appalling conditions or got out. The establishment of a women's section by the main labour organization, the Yūaikai, in 1916 acknowledged that women workers were a substantial element in the labour force, but for the most part little effort was made to organize female workers. The perspective that female workers were short term, uncommitted members of the workforce with little to gain from organization, in conjunction with the view that their sex rendered organization effectively impossible, made for a very low unionization rate.

The socialist political movement was no more successful in absorbing women into its ranks, although the legal ban on political activity did not prevent women from being informally involved with left-wing organizations. The Heiminsha of 1903–5 claimed an interest in women's rights, and socialist women's organizations, often with proletarian party associations, existed during the 1920s. A series of women played a prominent part in the movement—Fukuda Hideko, Kanno Suga (executed with anarchist Kōtoku Shūsui in 1911), Itō Noe, Yamakawa Kikue—but the disinterest of male socialist and labour leaders often drove them to sacrifice feminist concerns to what were considered the broader interests of the whole movement. As in other countries, male unionists feared women's advancement in the workplace; women encountered immense hostility to concepts such as equal work opportunities, equal wages and abolition of the patriarchal family system which threatened men's established hegemony. Socialist leaders continued to rely on the automatic liberation of women which they believed would accompany the advent of a socialist society. The activities of the few socialist women interested in women's rights and improving the lot of women workers were doomed to meet apathy, if not outright opposition, from male colleagues. Moreover, the socialist and non-socialist wings of the women's movement rarely came together in a united front.

Emphasis on Duties

Dynamic though many of these individuals were, the numbers interested in women's rights, labour and socialist activity paled into insignificance by comparison with the strength of the mass women's organizations, the first of which was the Patriotic Women's Association. These expanded rapidly in the 1920s and 1930s. The Patriotic Women's Association claimed three million members by the late 1930s, the army-sponsored National Defence Women's Association, formed in 1932, around eight million. Both had numerous local branches. These organizations were concerned not with women's rights, but with women's duties. Their task was the reinforcement of the patriarchal 'family state', and both became vehicles for the mobilization of the female population by the state for the purposes of war. They had a major impact on the lives of the majority, while agitation by the few non-establishment organizations and individuals seemed no more than peripheral to the concerns of most women.

Notwithstanding innate conservatism and the official reassertion of the traditional status of women, changing economic and labour market forces continued to exert a substantial influence on women's lives. Apart from their significance as wives, mothers and teachers, women continued to make up a large proportion of the workforce in the agricultural, industrial and commercial sectors. The agricultural smallholdings and tenancies which still sustained over 40 per cent of the population in the late 1930s became increasingly dependent on the labour contribution of the women of the family, both in the work of cultivation and in by-employment inside or outside the home. This process was accelerated by the absorbtion of men into the rapidly expanding industrial sector in the late 1930s, and into the armed forces.

Working the Farms

By 1940 women comprised over half the agricultural labour force (around seven million workers). This marked a reversal of the pattern earlier in the interwar years, when agricultural depression, climatic fluctuations and increasing population pressure on the land meant that poverty became increasingly severe in some villages. A woman's labour contribution was often considered less valuable to the farm, and the income she brought in had always been viewed as supplementary to the family budget. Thus in times of difficulty young women regarded as little more than

extra mouths to feed tended to be among the first to be shed by
the farm economy. More and more women and girls were forced
to search for alternative sources of income at a time when industrial depression meant that employment opportunities outside
the agricultural sector were declining. Male control over the female labour market weakened women's position still further.
Since girls had no independent legal status, they had from the
Meiji period been despatched to work in factories on the basis
of contracts signed by their fathers or elder brothers, with or
without the consent of the girl concerned. Although women became increasingly independent of their families in matters of employment in the 1920s and 1930s, they were still largely subject
to legal and economic control by the males of the household. In
the early 1930s girls from the depressed areas of the northeast
were not infrequently sent into prostitution by their parents because no other employment was available. Brothel-keepers, like
mill owners, paid a lump sum advance on wages to the head of
the family—crucial to tide it over current difficulties—but the
woman was in return committed to many years of service, if not
life-long bondage. The effective 'sale' of female labour exacer-
bated by the depression demonstrated that under the law women
were little higher than slaves and little more than chattels.

Their weak position at the bottom of the hierarchy made
women particularly vulnerable to the impact of economic difficulties, but far from increasing the agitation for change by
women, these harsh realities served to reinforce a broader sense
of frustration and despair. While women's interests might have
come to the fore in a time of prosperity they were now over-
taken by the broader discontent among the working classes.
Women's rights agitation was a luxury that could not be afforded;
repression was certain and there were more immediate economic
imperatives. In any case, for the mass of women local conservatism combined with efficient indoctrination and organization
by the authorities to pre-empt any thought of feminist protest.

Growing Opportunities

For some women the interwar years brought new opportunities.
The number engaged in clerical and non-manual occupations
grew apace. While the number of women employed in industry
grew only marginally, those working in the tertiary sector expanded by over 70 per cent to nearly 3.4 million between 1920

and 1940. Around half of these were in the service industries. Women advanced further in the professions. The barriers to women's entering such careers as medicine and the law were slowly removed. Women teachers became increasingly responsible for the early education of children. Though poorly represented at higher educational levels, even in girls' schools, they accounted for nearly half of all elementary school teachers by the 1930s.

THE HISTORY OF NATIONS
Chapter 4

Rise and Fall of the Japanese Empire

A Flawed Democracy Falters

By Noel F. Busch

Japan took on the appearance of a democracy with its 1889 constitution, proclaimed in the name of Emperor Meiji. For decades thereafter, real power remained with the emperor and a clique of advisers and cabinet members drawn from the samurai. As the Meiji generation died out, however, representative democracy became a more vibrant force, especially following World War I. But other forces were also at work in Japan, and as historian Noel F. Busch describes, by the 1930s these reduced the Diet, Japan's parliament, to a rubber stamp.

Seagoing people tend to be inherently adventurous souls who welcome new places, new people, and quite frequently, even new ideas. In naval officers this characteristic is likely to be nurtured by their voyages around the rest of the world, which help them pick up valuable pointers about human nature in general and the capabilities of potential enemies in particular. Army training conversely takes place mostly at home and seems to encourage, or at least to confirm, a more rigid and parochial outlook whereby alien viewpoints are impatiently brushed aside or simply ignored. In Japan during the twenties and thirties, such disparities between army and navy personnel, accentuated by outside circumstances, helped give competition, first between the two services and then between rival factions within the army, a decisive importance.

Weak Parliament

While the Meiji Constitution promulgated by the emperor in 1889 provided for a bicameral Diet, this body, prior to the 1920s, had never exerted an influence commensurate with that of parliamentary institutions in Great Britain or the United States. In Japan actual power had resided in a cabinet composed, during the later years of the Meiji era, of worthy successors to the able young samurai advisers who had counseled the emperor at the beginning of his reign. Of even the more recent Meiji dignitaries, however, only a few had survived their ruler, and by the mid-twenties, the only one of the so-called *genro*, or elder statesmen, who remained was the venerable Prince Saionji who lived on through the thirties. Meanwhile, the old emperor himself had been succeeded by an unreliable son whose antic attitude toward his largely ceremonial duties sometimes led to alarming innovations in governmental procedures. On one famous occasion, when handed a parchment scroll from which to read off a message to the Diet, he amused himself instead by rolling it up into a make-believe telescope through which he peered playfully about the chamber.

In 1921, two years before the [Great Kanto] earthquake [which destroyed much of Tokyo], Emperor Taisho's obvious unsuitability for office made it necessary to appoint as regent his son, Hirohito, the latter whose reign name was to be Showa. Hirohito was a well-meaning and intelligent young man who, however, also lacked most of Emperor Meiji's enthusiasm and aptitude for rule. Under the tutelage of Admiral Togo, he had responded to his mentor's nautical bias by developing an intense interest in, not the navy, but marine biology. In this field, he achieved scholarly distinction which, however, did little to compensate for his disinterest in terrestrial politics.

Toward Stronger Democracy

One of the conclusions drawn by Japan from the victory of the Allies in World War I was that democracy was a stronger and hence more desirable form of government than autocracy, as represented by the Central Powers. The result was a sudden lurch toward truly representative government accomplished during the early twenties through bills providing first for wider, and then, in 1925, for universal, male suffrage. However, while this made it seem possible that Japan's Diet would eventually move into the power vacuum created by the demise of Meiji and the genro, the Constitution contained at least two weaknesses which effectively precluded this possibility.

One weakness was that, while the Diet had the right to endorse or reject the budgets presented by the Cabinet, it did not have the right to substitute a new one of its own. This meant that, in the event of rejection, the budget of the previous year would remain operative. Since the main outlay was usually for the armed forces, this gave the military a disproportionate hold on the nation's purse strings.

The second weakness was that, while the emperor was the constitutional source of all power in the state, both armed services as well as the Diet itself were considered to be equally, and independently, representative of that power. Hence, if the army took an action not approved by the Diet, it could and, as things turned out, frequently did, claim to be acting on an interpretation of the emperor's wishes quite as valid as any that could be supplied by mere politicians. An emperor like Hirohito's grandfather might, to be sure, have clarified his wishes so emphatically as to remove all doubts about their interpretation, but such a course would have been wholly out of character for Hirohito.

During the early twenties, and even after the initiation of universal male suffrage, numerous superficial clues suggested that despite these constitutional flaws, Japan might well be on the threshold of genuine Western-style democracy. Western games like tennis, golf, and even American baseball became widely popular. Social customs changed enough to allow women to work in offices or, for that matter, as hostesses in dance halls or waitresses in Western-style restaurants. Western dress became increasingly popular, along with Western movies, music, and architecture—especially in Tokyo where massive steel and concrete buildings replaced wooden structures in wide areas destroyed by the postearthquake fires. What was more to the point was that these perhaps superficial indices had a solid economic substructure.

Vast Business Combines

During the Meiji period, Japan's financial and commercial community had developed rapidly and along peculiarly Japanese lines, in which family connections and clan loyalties were closely interwoven. Most typically Japanese of the evolving commercial institutions were naturally the biggest and most influential—the huge corporate structures called *zaibatsu* which, by the second decade of the twentieth century, had come to dominate the business scene in a fashion unparalleled in the West by even the biggest corporate giants. Each of the four major combines—Mitsui, Mitsubishi, Sumitomo, and Yasuda—while controlled by a single family, comprised thousands of employees. Each was involved in dozens of separate but interrelated enterprises, rather like what are nowadays known in the United States as "conglomerates" except that in Japan the conglomerations were even more heterogeneous.

The political influence of the zaibatsu upon the two major political parties, through friendly and familial relations with the Diet and the Cabinet, was naturally substantial. However, the essential point was not so much that one party might be inclined to favor the interests of the Mitsui while the other favored those of the Mitsubishi. Rather it was that all of the zaibatsu—and with them most of the important banks and the business community as a whole—were increasingly disposed to view the Diet rather than the armed forces as the institution most capable of directing the affairs of the nation.

During the twenties, Japan's business leaders had become increasingly inclined to doubt the pre–World War I theory, still held by the military, that what Japan needed was a colonial empire in China as a source of raw materials and a captive market for the products to be made out of them. Surely it would be far less costly, and far less provoking to valued clients in the Western world, simply to buy raw materials and then build up a worldwide export trade based on Japan's capacity to manufacture goods more cheaply than the West could. And if it were really possible for Japan thus to achieve economic security by peaceful means, why go to all the trouble and expense of conquest?

Themselves a relatively new force in the nation, Japan's business leaders were by no means eager to surrender their recently acquired status and influence to the military, especially the army with its enthusiasm for huge expenditures for armaments and its priority claims upon the labor force. All in all, as big business became more and more integrated with the political establishment, it began to seem entirely conceivable that Japan would be able to prosper by peaceful means despite a burgeoning population that, already well over sixty million, was still growing at the rate of one million a year.

The Depression Hits

What prevented the realization of this happy outcome was primarily the onset of the Great Depression which, in Japan, was superimposed on a domestic slump that had started in 1927. Hurt first by the reduced buying power of her foreign clients and then by protective tariffs imposed by them upon her products, Japan lacked the natural resources that gave most Western nations, and especially the United States, the self-sufficiency to ride out the storm. As the thirties began, the consensus of the business community in general and eventually even that of the zaibatsu veered back to the thesis underlying her territorial expansion before and during World War I, to which the army leaders had adhered throughout.

An additional factor in the equation now, and one which derived new weight from the onset of the Depression, was the threat of Communism as embodied by the U.S.S.R. Always suspicious of Russia—and, during the imperial era, not without good cause—Japan was now especially alert to conditions in China where Chiang Kai-shek was fighting a loose coalition of unpredictable war lords on the one hand and Mao Tse-tung's Communist forces on the other. The threat of a Communist take-over in China which would menace Japan's interests in Korea helped accelerate the shifting balance of political forces within Japan and the change in Japanese policy that derived from it.

Seizing Manchuria

The first substantive results of this profound change came in September of 1931, when Japanese army units stationed in Manchuria ostensibly to safeguard the South Manchurian Railway which Japan had acquired from Russia a quarter of a century before, suddenly felt themselves obliged to take over the entire area comprising some 400,000 square miles and a population of some 30 million. While they apparently did so without the knowledge, let alone the approval, of their government, what was even more indicative of the new sentiment in Japan was that neither the army high command nor the government saw fit to rescind the occupation or even to rebuke the unit commanders concerned. Instead, they endorsed the take-overs the following year by providing Manchuria with the new name of Manchukuo and a young puppet emperor in the person of Henry Pu-yi, heir to the Manchu dynasty that had been ousted from Peking by the revolution of 1911. One result of this feat was to give Japan a major overseas source of raw materials. Another—since the feat had been accomplished at negligible human or monetary cost—was widespread acceptance of the army as the true warden of national welfare. When the League of Nations denounced the action and withheld recognition of the new state, Japan responded by blandly withdrawing from that august organization. Protests from the United States—whose stand on tariffs and immigration were hardly calculated to have ensured a sympathetic hearing on such matters—were likewise politely ignored.

After what Japan was thereafter to refer to as "the Manchurian Incident," the question was not whether Japan was to have a two-party system of parliamentary government, much less which of the two parties was to win election. It was merely which one of the two contending factions in the army was to determine the destiny of the nation.

The Militarists Take Power

By Robert L. Worden

The growth of democracy in the 1920s, which began with the extension of voting rights to all adult males in Japan, ran into violent opposition from ultranationalists and militarists. Assassinations, coup attempts, and an Imperial Army determined to chart its own course in Asia combined to undermine representative government. In this selection from a Library of Congress study of Japan, historian Robert L. Worden traces the foreign and domestic pressures that led to a military seizure of power in the late 1920s and early 1930s.

T he two-party political system that had been developing in Japan since the turn of the century finally came of age after World War I. This period has sometimes been called that of "Taishō democracy," after the reign title of the emperor. In 1918 Hara Takashi (1856–1921), a protégé of Saionji and a major influence in the prewar Seiyūkai cabinets, had become the first commoner to serve as prime minister. He took advantage of long-standing relationships he had throughout the government, won the support of the surviving *genrō* and the House of Peers, and brought into his cabinet as army minister Tanaka Giichi (1864–1929), who had a greater appreciation of favorable civil-military relations than his predecessors. Nevertheless, major problems confronted Hara: inflation, the need to adjust the Japanese economy to postwar circumstances, the influx of foreign ideas, and an emerging labor movement. Prewar solutions were applied by the cabinet to these postwar problems, and little was done to reform the government. Hara worked to ensure a Seiyūkai majority through time-tested methods, such as new election laws and electoral redistricting, and embarked on major government-funded public works programs.

Ronald E. Dolan and Robert L. Worden, *Japan: A Country Study*. Washington, DC: U.S. Government Press, 1992.

The public grew disillusioned with the growing national debt and the new election laws, which retained the old minimum tax qualifications for voters. Calls were raised for universal suffrage and the dismantling of the old political party network. Students, university professors, and journalists, bolstered by labor unions and inspired by a variety of democratic, socialist, communist, anarchist, and other Western schools of thought, mounted large but orderly public demonstrations in favor of universal male suffrage in 1919 and 1920. New elections brought still another Seiyūkai majority, but barely so. In the political milieu of the day, there was a proliferation of new parties, including socialist and communist parties.

In the midst of this political ferment, Hara was assassinated by a disenchanted railroad worker in 1921. He was followed by a succession of nonparty prime ministers and coalition cabinets. Fear of a broader electorate, left-wing power, and the growing social change engendered by the influx of Western popular culture together led to the passage of the Peace Preservation Law (1925), which forbade any change in the political structure or the abolition of private property.

Unstable coalitions and divisiveness in the Diet led the Kenseikai (Constitutional Government Association) and the Seiyū Hontō (True Seiyūkai) to merge as the Rikken Minseitō (Constitutional Democratic Party) in 1927. The Minseitō platform was committed to the parliamentary system, democratic politics, and world peace. Thereafter, until 1932, the Seiyūkai and the Rikken Minseitō alternated in power.

Rising Discontent

Despite the political realignments and hope for more orderly government, domestic economic crises plagued whichever party held power. Fiscal austerity programs and appeals for public support of conservative government policies like the Peace Preservation Law—including reminders of the moral obligation to make sacrifices for the emperor and the state—were attempted as solutions. Although the world depression of the late 1920s and early 1930s had minimal effects on Japan—indeed Japanese exports grew substantially during this period—there was a sense of rising discontent that was heightened with the assassination of Minseitō prime minister Hamaguchi Osachi in 1931.

The events flowing from the Meiji Restoration in 1868 had seen not only the fulfillment of many domestic and foreign economic and political objectives—without Japan's first suffering the colonial fate of other Asian nations—but also a new intellectual ferment, in a time when there was interest worldwide in socialism and an urban proletariat was developing. Universal male suffrage, social welfare, workers' rights, and nonviolent protest were ideals of the early leftist movement. Government suppression of leftist activities, however, led to more radical leftist action and even more suppression, resulting in the dissolution of the Japan Socialist Party (Nihon Shakaitō), only a year after its 1906 founding, and in the general failure of the socialist movement.

The victory of the communists in Russia in 1917 and their hopes for a world revolution led to the establishment of the Comintern (a contraction of Communist International, the organization founded in Moscow in 1919 to coordinate the world communist movement). The Comintern realized the importance of Japan in achieving successful revolution in East Asia and actively worked to form the Japan Communist Party (Nihon Kyōsantō), which was founded in July 1922. An end to feudalism, the abolition of the monarchy, withdrawal of Japanese troops from Siberia, Sakhalin, China, Korea, and Taiwan, and recognition of the Soviet Union were the announced goals of the Japan Communist Party in 1923. A brutal suppression of the party followed. Radicals responded with an assassination attempt on Prince Regent Hirohito. The 1925 Peace Preservation Law was a direct response to the "dangerous thoughts" perpetrated by communist elements in Japan.

The liberalization of election laws, also in 1925, benefited communist candidates even though the Japan Communist Party itself was banned. A new Peace Preservation Law in 1928, however, further impeded communist efforts by banning the parties they had infiltrated. The police apparatus of the day was ubiquitous and quite thorough in attempting to control the socialist movement. By 1926 the Japan Communist Party had been forced underground, by the summer of 1929 the party leadership had been virtually destroyed, and by 1933 the party had largely disintegrated.

Diplomatic Challenges

Emerging Chinese nationalism, the victory of the communists in Russia, and the growing presence of the United States in East Asia all worked against Japan's postwar foreign policy interests.

The four-year Siberian expedition and activities in China, combined with big domestic spending programs, had depleted Japan's wartime earnings. Only through more competitive business practices, supported by further economic development and industrial modernization, all accommodated by the growth of the *zaibatsu*, could Japan hope to become predominant in Asia. The United States, long a source of many imported goods and loans needed for development, was seen as becoming a major impediment to this goal because of its policies of containing Japanese imperialism.

An international turning point in military diplomacy was the Washington Conference of 1921–22, which produced a series of agreements that effected a new order in the Pacific region. Japan's economic problems made a naval buildup nearly impossible and, realizing the need to compete with the United States on an economic rather than a military basis, the Japanese government came to see rapprochement as inevitable. Japan adopted a more neutral attitude toward the civil war in China; joined the United States, Britain, and France in encouraging Chinese self-development; and dropped efforts to expand its hegemony into China proper.

A Series of Treaties

In the Four Power Treaty on Insular Possessions (December 13, 1921), Japan, the United States, Britain, and France agreed to recognize the status quo in the Pacific, and Japan and Britain agreed to terminate formally their Treaty of Alliance. The Five Power Naval Disarmament Treaty (February 6, 1922) established an international capital ship ratio (5, 5, 3, 1.75, and 1.75, respectively, for the United States, Britain, Japan, France, and Italy) and limited the size and armaments of capital ships already built or under construction. In a move that gave the Japanese Imperial Navy greater freedom in the Pacific, Washington and London agreed not to build any new military bases between Singapore and Hawaii.

The goal of the Nine Power Treaty (February 6, 1922), signed by Belgium, China, the Netherlands, and Portugal along with the original five powers, was the prevention of war in the Pacific. The signatories agreed to respect China's independence and integrity, not to interfere in Chinese attempts to establish a stable government, to refrain from seeking special privileges in China or threatening the positions of other nations there, to support a policy of equal opportunity for commerce and industry of all nations in China, and to reexamine extraterritoriality and tariff autonomy policies. Japan also agreed to withdraw its troops from Shandong, relinquishing all but purely economic rights there, and to evacuate its troops from Siberia.

In 1928 Japan joined fourteen other nations in signing the Kellogg-Briand Pact, which denounced "recourse to war for the solution of international controversies." Thus, when Japan invaded Manchuria only three years later, its pretext was the defense of its nationals and economic interests there. The London Naval Conference in 1930 came at the time of an economic recession in Japan, and the Japanese government was amenable to further, cost-saving naval reductions. Although Prime Minister Hamaguchi Osachi (1870–1931) had civilian support, he bypassed the Naval General Staff and approved the signing of the London Naval Treaty. Hamaguchi's success was pyrrhic: ultranationalists called the treaty a national surrender, and navy and army officials girded themselves for defense of their budgets. Hamaguchi himself died from wounds suffered in an assassination attempt in November 1930, and the treaty, with its complex formula for ship tonnage and numbers aimed at restricting the naval arms race, had loopholes that made it ineffective by 1938.

Ultranationalism had characterized right-wing politicians and conservative military men since the inception of the Meiji Restoration, contributing greatly to the prowar politics of the 1870s. Disenchanted former samurai had formed patriotic societies and intelligence-gathering organizations, such as the Gen'yōha (Black Ocean Society, founded in 1881) and its later offshoot, the Kokuryūkai (Black Dragon Society, or Amur River Society, founded in 1901). These groups became active in domestic and foreign politics, helped foment prowar sentiments, and supported ultranationalist causes through the end of World War II. After Japan's victories over China and Russia, the ultranationalists concentrated on domestic issues and perceived domestic threats, such as socialism and communism.

Emperor Worship

After World War I and the intellectual ferment of the period, nationalist societies became numerous but had a minority voice during the era of two-party democratic politics. Diverse and angry groups called for nationalization of all wealth above a fixed minimal amount and for armed overseas expansion. The emperor was highly revered by these groups, and when Hirohito was enthroned in 1927 initiating the Shōwa period (Bright Harmony, 1926–89), there were calls for a "Shōwa Restoration" and a revival of Shinto. Emperor-centered neo-Shintoism, or State Shinto, which had long been developing, came to fruition in the 1930s and 1940s. It glorified the emperor and traditional Japanese virtues to the exclusion of the Western influences perceived as greedy, individualistic, bourgeois, and assertive. The ideals of the Japanese family-state and self-sacrifice in service of the nation were given a missionary interpretation, being thought by their ultranationalist proponents to be applicable to the modern world.

The 1930s were a decade of fear in Japan, characterized by the resurgence of right-wing patriotism, the weakening of democratic forces, domestic terrorist violence (including an assassination attempt on the emperor in 1932), and stepped-up military aggression abroad. A prelude to this state of affairs was Tanaka Giichi's term as prime minister from 1927 to 1929. Twice he sent troops to China to obstruct Chiang Kai-shek's unification campaign, and, in June 1928, adventurous officers of the Guandong Army, the Imperial Japanese Army unit stationed in Manchuria, embarked on unauthorized initiatives to protect Japanese interests, including the assassination of a former ally, Manchurian warlord Zhang Zuolin. The perpetrators hoped the Chinese would be prompted to take military action, forcing the Guandong Army to retaliate. The Japanese high command and the Chinese, however, both refused to mobilize. The incident turned out to be a striking example of unchecked terrorism. Even though press censorship kept the Japanese public from knowing about these events, they led to the downfall of Tanaka and set the stage for a similar plot, the Manchurian Incident, in 1931.

Plotting a Takeover

A secret society founded by army officers seeking to establish a military dictatorship—the Sakurakai (Cherry Society, the cherry blossom being emblematic of self-sacrifice)—plotted to attack the Diet and political party headquarters, assassinate the prime minister, and declare martial law under a "Shōwa Restoration" government led by the army minister. Although the army cancelled its coup plans (to have been carried out in March 1931), no reprisals were taken and terrorist activity was again tacitly condoned.

The Manchurian Incident of September 1931 did not fail and

it set the stage for the eventual military takeover of the Japanese government. Guandong Army conspirators blew up a few meters of South Manchurian Railway Company track near Mukden (now Shenyang), blamed it on Chinese saboteurs, and used the event as an excuse to seize Mukden. One month later, in Tokyo, military figures plotted the October Incident, which was aimed at setting up a national socialist state. The plot failed, but again the news was suppressed and the military perpetrators were not punished. Japanese forces attacked Shanghai in January 1932 on the pretext of Chinese resistance in Manchuria. Finding stiff Chinese resistance in Shanghai, the Japanese waged a three-month undeclared war there before a truce was reached in March 1932. Several days later, Manchukuo was established. Manchukuo was a Japanese puppet state headed by the last Chinese emperor, Puyi, as chief executive and later emperor. The civilian government in Tokyo was powerless to prevent these military happenings. Instead of being condemned, the Guandong Army's actions enjoyed popular support back home. International reactions were extremely negative, however. Japan withdrew from the League of Nations, and the United States became increasingly hostile.

The Japanese system of party government finally met its demise with the May 15th Incident in 1932, when a group of junior naval officers and army cadets assassinated Prime Minister Inukai Tsuyoshi (1855–1932). Although the assassins were put on trial and sentenced to fifteen years' imprisonment, they were seen popularly as having acted out of patriotism. Inukai's successors, military men chosen by Saionji, the last surviving *genrō* [elder statesman] recognized Manchukuo and generally approved the army's actions in securing Manchuria as an industrial base, an area for Japanese emigration, and a staging ground for war with the Soviet Union. Various army factions contended for power amid increasing suppression of dissent and more assassinations. In the February 26th Incident of 1936, about 1,500 troops went on a rampage of assassination against the current and former prime ministers and other cabinet members, and even Saionji and members of the imperial court. The revolt was put down by other military units and its leaders executed after secret trials. Despite public dismay over these events and the discredit they brought to numerous military figures, Japan's civilian leadership capitulated to the army's demands in the hope of ending domestic violence. Increases were seen in defense budgets, naval construction (Japan announced it would no longer accede to the London Naval Treaty), and patriotic indoctrination as Japan moved toward a wartime footing.

In November 1936, the Anti-Comintern Pact, an agreement to exchange information and collaborate in preventing communist activities, was signed by Japan and Germany (Italy joined a year later). War was launched against China after the Marco Polo Bridge Incident of July 7, 1937, in which an allegedly unplanned clash took place near Beiping (as Beijing was then called) between Chinese and Japanese troops and quickly escalated into full-scale warfare. The Second Sino-Japanese War (1937–45) ensued, and relations with the United States, Britain, and the Soviet Union deteriorated. The increased military activities in China—and Japan's idea of establishing "Mengukuo" in Inner Mongolia and the Mongolian People's Republic—soon led to a major clash over rival Mongolia-Manchukuo border claims. When Japanese troops invaded eastern Mongolia, a major ground and air battle with a joint Soviet-Mongolian army took place between May and September 1939 at the Battle of Halhin Gol. The Japanese were severely defeated, sustaining as many as 80,000 casualties, and thereafter Japan concentrated its war efforts on its southward drive in China and Southeast Asia, a strategy that helped propel Japan ever closer to war with the United States, Britain, and their allies.

Under the prime ministership of Konoe Fumimaro (1891–1945)—the last head of the famous Fujiwara house—the government was streamlined and given absolute power over the nation's assets. In 1940, the 2,600th anniversary of the founding of Japan according to tradition, Konoe's cabinet called for the establishment of a "Greater East Asia Coprosperity Sphere," a concept building on Konoe's 1938 call for a "New Order in Greater East Asia," encompassing Japan, Manchukuo, China, and Southeast Asia. The Greater East Asia Coprosperity Sphere was to integrate Asia politically and economically—under Japanese leadership—against Western domination. It was developed in recognition of the changing geopolitical situation emerging in 1940, and, eventually, a Greater East Asia Ministry was established (in 1942) and the Greater East Asia Conference was held in Tokyo in 1943. Also in 1940, political parties were ordered to dissolve, and the Imperial Rule Assistance Association, comprising members of all former parties, was established to transmit government orders throughout society.

The Pacific War

By Milton W. Meyer

*Throughout the 1930s, Japan struggled to recover from the Great De-
pression. Just as in Weimar Germany, economic woes inspired violent
right-wing movements in Japan and encouraged the Imperial Army to
adventurism in China. As the Nazis plunged Europe into war in 1939,
Japan saw an opportunity to gain allies in its struggles with the Rus-
sians, British, Dutch, and Americans for control of Asian territory and resources. In 1940, the militaristic government of Japan threw its lot in
with Nazi Germany and fascist Italy. A year later, the Pacific War
opened with a Japanese attack on Pearl Harbor. In this excerpt from*
Japan: A Concise History, *author Milton W. Meyer recounts the major
events surrounding the Pacific theater of World War II.*

In September 1940, after the fall of France and fresh German
successes in Europe, the three states [Germany, Italy, and
Japan] concluded the Tripartite, or Axis, Pact, directed essentially against the United States. Its terms provided that if one of
the three contracting states were to be attacked by a power not
then involved in the European war or the Chinese-Japanese conflict, the other two signatories would assist the partner with all
political, economic, and military means. Because at the time only
the United States and the Soviet Union, among the major states,
were neutral, another article of the treaty stated that the terms
did not affect the status then existing between each of the three
parties and the Soviet Union. Despite these multilateral treaty
arrangements, Japan's relationship with the Axis powers in Europe was not a happy one. They were never really united in common outlook and planning. The European and Asian parties
went their respective, separate ways, and each neglected to inform
the other of basic war plans and strategies.

Japan endeavored to secure its northern flank from Soviet advances. In 1935, the Soviet Union sold the Chinese Eastern Rail-

road to Japan and kept out of Manchuria and China. But on several occasions, largescale military clashes along mutual Asian borders erupted between Japan and its neighbor. Between 1937 and 1939, fighting broke out over islands in the Amur River, which formed much of the Manchurian-Siberian border, at Zhangufang (Changkufeng) Hill near the Korean-Manchurian border, and in the Nomonhan border region in Inner Mongolia. Tens of thousands of troops were employed in these campaigns, especially the last one, by both sides, but war was not declared. Then, with the conclusion of the surprising and unexpected German-Soviet neutrality pact between Hitler and Stalin signed in July 1939, Japan, fearing a Soviet attack, halted its aggressive action. Two years later, when Hitler, unilaterally ending the treaty, attacked the Soviet Union, Japan felt safer and it redirected efforts southward. Japanese military counsels decided against moving into eastern Siberia with its relative paucity of known natural resources at the time, including a lack of oil, essential for military and industrial operations. But to make doubly sure of Soviet intentions, Japan concluded with the Soviet Union in April 1941, a five-year neutrality pact in which each party pledged not to go to war with the other during that interim.

Japan Overruns China

Japan meanwhile had expanded its military operations along the farflung Chinese coastal areas and plains. On July 7, 1937, at Luguoqiao (Lukuochiao, the so-called Marco Polo Bridge) near Peking, shots were exchanged between the Chinese garrison and Japanese forces on maneuvers there, where they had no treaty right to be. Although the Chinese apologized, the tense situation persisted, and the Japanese military used the incident, one of any number that had broken out in the area, as a pretext for continued expansion.

Now there was no stopping Japan's military advances in China in these pre–Pearl Harbor years (1937–1941), known as the China Incident. By the end of July, Japanese troops occupied Peking. They fanned out over the northern China plain until they were met and contained by the independently operating Chinese Communist guerrilla armies near the last great bend of the Yellow River. In central China, along the broad Yangzi River in another operation, the Japanese, in 1937 and 1938, also spread out from Shanghai, where they, like other, major Western, powers, had extensive economic interests and troops protecting them. The Japanese captured Chiang Kai-shek's capital of Nanjing, where they massacred inhabitants and proceeded up the broad river valley. The Nationalist Chinese regime fled upstream to Chongqing (Chungking), located in the Yangzi River gorges nearly impregnable to invading enemy land forces. Chongqing

THE ATTACK ON PEARL HARBOR

Japan's surprise attack on the U.S. fleet at Pearl Harbor near the end of 1941 gave it supremacy in the Pacific for the next five months. The U.S. Navy's Naval Historical Center offers a brief account of the attack and its consequences.

The 7 December 1941 Japanese raid on Pearl Harbor was one of the great defining moments in history. A single carefully-planned and well-executed stroke removed the United States Navy's battleship force as a possible threat to the Japanese Empire's southward expansion. America, unprepared and now considerably weakened, was abruptly brought into the Second World War as a full combatant.

Eighteen months earlier, President Franklin D. Roosevelt had transferred the United States Fleet to Pearl Harbor as a presumed deterrent to Japanese aggression. The Japanese military, deeply engaged in the seemingly endless war it had started against China in mid-1937, badly needed oil and other raw materials. Commercial access to these was gradually curtailed as the conquests continued. In July 1941 the Western powers effectively halted trade with Japan. From then on, as the desperate Japanese schemed to seize the oil and mineral-rich East Indies and Southeast Asia, a Pacific war was virtually inevitable.

By late November 1941, with peace negotiations clearly approaching an end, informed U.S. officials (and they were well-informed, they believed, through an ability to read Japan's diplomatic codes) fully expected a Japanese attack into the Indies, Malaya and probably the Philippines. Com-

remained Chiang's capital throughout the war years. In southern China, in a third operation, Japanese forces occupied the large city of Guangzhou (Canton) near Hong Kong and moved inland along narrow river valleys and railroad lines. They occupied coastal enclaves between Shanghai and Guangzhou but never penetrated the rugged hilly terrain of interior southcoastal China.

pletely unanticipated was the prospect that Japan would attack east, as well.

The U.S. Fleet's Pearl Harbor base was reachable by an aircraft carrier force, and the Japanese Navy secretly sent one across the Pacific with greater aerial striking power than had ever been seen on the World's oceans. Its planes hit just before 8AM on 7 December. Within a short time five of eight battleships at Pearl Harbor were sunk or sinking, with the rest damaged. Several other ships and most Hawaii-based combat planes were also knocked out and over 2400 Americans were dead. Soon after, Japanese planes eliminated much of the American air force in the Philippines, and a Japanese Army was ashore in Malaya.

These great Japanese successes, achieved without prior diplomatic formalities, shocked and enraged the previously divided American people into a level of purposeful unity hardly seen before or since. For the next five months, until the Battle of the Coral Sea in early May, Japan's far-reaching offensives proceeded untroubled by fruitful opposition. American and Allied morale suffered accordingly. Under normal political circumstances, an accommodation might have been considered.

However, the memory of the "sneak attack" on Pearl Harbor fueled a determination to fight on. Once the Battle of Midway in early June 1942 had eliminated much of Japan's striking power, that same memory stoked a relentless war to reverse her conquests and remove her, and her German and Italian allies, as future threats to World peace.

Naval Historical Center, "Pearl Harbor Raid, 7 December 1941." www. history.navy.mil.

Several years prior to Pearl Harbor, the Japanese in China had absorbed most of the Chinese territory they were ever to secure. No formal declaration of war followed any of these Japanese military operations. As in the case of Manchuria, Japan tried to set up puppet governments in occupied China. In December 1937, it established in Beijing, a traditional capital of later Chinese dynasties, the provisional Government of the Republic of China with elderly, experienced Chinese, hostile to Chiang Kai-shek's regime, as head officials. But the Japanese desired some outstanding Chinese to form a national government that could be recognized as legitimate for all China. They brought pressure to bear on a few warlords without success until they managed to obtain the services of Wang Jingwei (Wang Ching-wei), who had held high civilian positions under Chiang Kai-shek, but who had become dissatisfied with a perennially secondary position to the generalissimo.

In March 1940, the Japanese proclaimed the return of the national government to Nanjing under Wang, who remained subservient to the Japanese until his death in 1944. The Japanese gave diplomatic recognition to his government and concluded a treaty of friendship with it, which was eventually recognized by Japan's totalitarian associates in Europe. Political reorganization was accompanied by a new economic plan, the coprosperity sphere, enunciated earlier by the Japanese cabinet in 1938. Japanese companies and corporations controlled either directly or through subsidiaries the economic life of occupied China. Cultural redirection also was ordered. Schools were reorganized and textbooks were revised; history was rewritten. The Japanese attempted to impose total administration of subjugated areas. Through such wide-ranging and thorough policies, prior to the outbreak of the Pacific war in 1941, Japan was well versed in the establishment and techniques of managing puppet governments.

Japanese expansion infringed on Western rights, particularly those of Great Britain, which retained strong economic interests in occupied China. The Japanese disliked the British, who through Hong Kong and Burma permitted aid, albeit a trickle, to flow to the capital of free, unoccupied China at Chongqing. Walking a tightrope, the British, under Japanese pressure, closed the Burma Road for three months in mid-1940, but then reopened it. In China, British subjects and diplomats suffered indignities and maltreatment. The Japanese seemed to delight in insulting the British to reveal the latter's impotence to take retaliatory action. With comparatively few troops committed to Asia, particularly after the outbreak of the European war, the British were constricted in the possibilities of taking positive action, and the Japanese were well aware of this.

Similarly, the Japanese pushed into Indochina after the fall of France in June 1940 and met with little resistance there. With the conclusion of the Hanoi Convention later that year, Japan received the right to station troops in northern Indochina. In July 1941, Japanese troops marched into Saigon. For all intents and purposes, Japan also had occupied Indochina prior to Pearl Harbor. Coveting the valuable oil, rubber, and tin of Indonesia, after the fall of the Netherlands to the Nazis in spring 1940, Japan sent delegations to Batavia, the capital of the East Indies. The Dutch, more immune in their archipelago from the Japanese than the hapless French on the continent, refused to extend any concessions until their Asian possessions were occupied by the Japanese after the advent of open hostilities there in early 1942.

Japan and the United States

As the United States had done on previous occasions, it protested the infringement of its treaty rights in China. It refused to recognize the puppet Wang Jingwei and, for the record, continually protested individual and collective private and official insults and attacks by the Japanese. . . .

In July 1938, the United States invoked a moral embargo, in effect an appeal to the consciences of exporters, on the sale of airplanes to Japanese importers because, it was argued, these planes, some with U.S.-made parts and using U.S. oil, were used to bomb hapless Chinese civilians. In December 1939, the moral embargoes were extended to cover shipments of oil and petroleum products to Japan. Earlier, in July of that year, the United States announced its intention to terminate the 1911 treaty of commerce, with its clauses of nondiscriminatory treatment. Japan's place in normal bilateral trade channels would then halt, and legal obstacles would be imposed should the United States desire to restrict further trade with Japan. Following this more effective policy, in the following July and December, stringent export controls were invoked on a worldwide basis. These controls particularly affected Japan, which relied on imports of U.S.

oil and items of war for its military machine. The import controls were imposed on scrap iron, aviation gas, munitions, and other implements of war. In July 1941, after the occupation by Japanese troops of Saigon following an American presidential warning, the United States froze Japanese financial assets and embargoed all oil exports, so essential to the dwindling stocks of the ever-expanding Japanese military machine. . . .

Against the backdrop of irreconcilable positions, Japan took the decision to go to war.

As early as July 2, 1941, an imperial conference decided on a drive into Southeast Asia, where valuable natural resources could be obtained. Subsequent conferences reiterated the strategy. In October, General Tojo Hideki, as one of the top-ranking Japanese militarists, became prime minister, and expansionist plans swung into action. On November 1, Admiral Yamamoto Isoroku issued the orders for an attack on Pearl Harbor, which was meant to immobilize the U.S. Pacific Fleet temporarily while the Japanese could consolidate their gains in Southeast Asia. On Novem-

DIARY OF A STUDENT VOLUNTEER FOR A SUICIDE MISSION

As the tide of war turned against Japan, it relied increasingly on suicide missions against the Allies. These included the famous kamikaze suicide fliers and seaborne "human torpedoes." Excerpts from the diary of a volunteer follow.

April 18, 1945. Exactly one month from today. I feel as if I am to take my final examination.

Exactly one more month, then we will be sent to the front to face our enemy. I am going to get after our enemy, and aside from this particular feeling, I have no thought of death.

We are lucky, we need not be bothered with questions like "what is life?" or "what is death?"

I cannot talk like a sub-lieutenant by the name of N who exaggerates everything. Every word that comes out of his

ber 17, the admiral designated December 7 as the attack date. On November 26, under Vice Admiral Nagumo Chuichi's command, the Pearl Harbor Striking Force, composed of dozens of vessels, including six carriers protected by two battleships, three cruisers, and nine destroyers, sortied from Etorufu in the Kuriles.

On the same day in Washington, [Secretary of State Cordell] Hull reiterated his final proposals for peace to a special Japanese delegation. On November 27, Washington, which had broken the secret Japanese diplomatic code (but not the military ones), sent war warnings to posts abroad, including Pearl Harbor. These warnings, however, indicated possible aggression in the Philippines or in Malaya, rather than in Hawaii. In the meantime, the Japanese striking force, undetected, approached Hawaii by a circuitous route across the north Pacific Ocean. In the early hours of Sunday, December 7, despite the sinking of a midget Japanese submarine and the fact that a U.S. army radar picked up on its screen planes that turned out to have been launched from Japanese carriers, the first Japanese air attack at 7:55 A.M. (and a

mouth is full of patriotism. In my placid mind now, all such thoughts are consigned to the depth of quiet reflection. Some people may say that this type of inner reflection is unwarranted at a time like this. However, we have discovered the meaning of thinking, and this is a burden we have to bear. I believe that only in bearing the burden of thinking will I be able to account for the meaning of my own life....

I once rose up courageously, then why do I still have room for this type of thought? Am I a coward?

My comrades in arms have said to me that my face has betrayed my weariness for the past several days.

I know during the same period I have been trying to give meaning to my own death.

I have been absorbed in the task of making an angle-of-fire chart so that I can make my human torpedo hit the enemy for sure. I am now making much fewer errors in judging azimuth angles.

David J. Lu, *Japan: A Documentary History.* Armonk, NY: M.E. Sharpe, Inc., 1997.

second assault forty-five minutes later) caught Hawaiian forces unprepared. In less than two hours, six U.S. battleships were disabled, 120 planes were destroyed, and 2,400 men, mainly naval personnel, were killed. Japanese losses were minimal. Pearl Harbor united a previously divided American people, but the first year of the Pacific war proved successful for the Japanese (who now escalated the China Incident into the Greater East Asia War, but postwar, it was called by many, as in the United States, the Pacific war). Japan won all major objectives in Asia and the Pacific, and in the flush of victory disease, it established control over land and sea areas from the Aleutians in the north to Indonesia in the south and from Burma in the west to the central Pacific archipelagoes. Japan's initial successes made a great psychological impact on Asian peoples, for an Asian country had defeated Western nations. The myth of the invincibility of the white man had again been exploded (as in the Russo-Japanese War), as he was paraded through Asian streets as a prisoner of war. Colonial regimes in Southeast Asia toppled, and native nationalism was given impetus. The Japanese set up autonomous indigenous governments that claimed independence from the colonial powers. But as the war wore on, friction developed between the Japanese and their sponsored native governments. By the end of the war, the Japanese, because of their many brutal and tactless actions, became as discredited as the earlier colonial powers. Asia for Asians turned out to be more appropriately Asia for the Japanese. The conquerors, who through their enunciated Greater East Asia Coprosperity Sphere ended white domination in East and Southeast Asia, had sought local support for this end; instead, they reaped a disenchanted populace.

Despite extensive losses at Pearl Harbor, the United States recovered and made use of its remaining fleet, including aircraft carriers, until U.S. industry could replace and augment the military losses. The British fleet was decimated, because Singapore, the important naval base, had been taken and the British battleships sunk. On the other hand, the Japanese navy was in prime condition, but it began to receive setbacks after initial victories through a combination of second-rate strategy and some bad luck. In the Battle of Coral Sea, May 4–8, 1942, off Australia, the Japanese tried to secure Port Moresby, on the southern coast of New Guinea, as a southern anchor point. It was a unique naval battle, because all fighting was done by carrier planes against enemy planes, or by planes against enemy ships. Turned back, the Japanese failed to take the port.

A Turning Point

The Battle of Midway (June 4–6, 1942) was conceived by Admiral Yamamoto as a frontal attack on Hawaiian positions. It was partially concealed by Japanese operations farther north in the Aleutians (where the United States temporarily lost Kiska and Attu islands). But Admiral Chester Nimitz, now taking advantage of decoded Japanese military messages, saturated the Japanese navy with air attacks from land- and carrier-based planes. The Japanese failed to gain Midway, and in the battle, which constituted the first major defeat of the Japanese navy, Japan lost four of its best aircraft carriers. Subsequently, in the south Pacific operations in the Solomon Islands, mainly Guadalcanal, the Japanese failed in their strategy to achieve a strong southern position in order to cut off the heavily used U.S.-Australian supply lines. The tide of war was changing in the Pacific. The Allied cause slowly advanced northward, island-hopping under General Douglas MacArthur. MacArthur had withdrawn from the Philippines early in 1942 to Australia, which became his headquarters and base of military operations, and moved Allied troops, chiefly U.S. and Australian, up the north New Guinea coast to capture Japanese outposts.

Complementing MacArthur's military drive up the southwest Pacific island chains, which aimed at retaking the Philippines, were engagements across the central Pacific Ocean under Admiral Nimitz, with principally naval action. In March 1943, the two Aleutian islands of Attu and Kiska were retaken. By mid-1944, intensive but costly operations in the Pacific regained the Gilberts, including Makin and Tarawa atolls, the Marshalls, including Kwajalein and Eniwetok; and finally the Marianas, among which were Guam, Saipan, and Tinian. The fall of Saipan in July 1944 proved a turning point in the Pacific war. From the Marianas, Japan could easily be reached in round-trip saturation bombing raids (fields in China were too distant for the same purpose). Tojo's cabinet fell in mid-1944, and in the course of the hectic war's end, it was succeeded by four others within a year into the days of surrender: Koiso Kuniaki, 1944–1945; Suzuki Kantaro, April 1945; Prince Higashi-kuni, August 1945; and Shidehara Kijuro, October 1945. Although no Japanese openly talked of defeat,

Japan's surprise attack on Pearl Harbor devastated the U.S. fleet.

some leaders were privately considering the possibility of a negotiated peace. The Allied troops, drawn from both the southwest and central Pacific theaters of operation, converged on the Philippines in October 1944. The final campaigns in the first half of 1945 included those at Iwo Jima and Okinawa, which were to be used as a staging area for the invasion of Japan. . . .

Complete Surrender Demanded

In January 1943, Roosevelt met with British Prime Minister Winston Churchill in Casablanca, where they issued the unconditional surrender statement. The Allies, they pledged, would fight until the unconditional surrender of their enemies in Europe and in Asia. There was to be no repetition of any of [President Woodrow] Wilson's Fourteen Points at Versailles implying accommodation of the enemy. The insistence on unconditional surrender was controversial, for it spurred the Japanese militarists to fight to the bitter end, in the absence of any other mitigating alternative. The demand probably delayed the Japanese surrender, for the army used it in their arguments against the foreign office and the navy to conclude peace. In the case of Japan, unconditional surrender turned out anyway to be conditional, for the Japanese requested and received the right to retain the emperor, who was made subject to the directives of General MacArthur, designated by the Allies as the Supreme Commander of the Allied Powers (SCAP) in Japan.

In November 1943, Roosevelt and Churchill met with Chiang Kai-shek at Cairo. There they agreed on the course of future operations against Japan and issued a joint statement of purpose. In the Cairo Declaration of November 26, four general areas of intent were announced. First, Japan was to be stripped of all islands in the Pacific seized or occupied since 1914. This essentially meant that the league mandates of the ex-German territories would be terminated. Second, all territories that Japan had "stolen" from China were to be returned to the Republic of China. These included Manchuria, other occupied areas on the continent, Taiwan, and the Pescadores. Third, Japan was to be expelled from all other territories taken by violence and greed. This covered much territory. It was understandable in terms of mainland and insular Asian holdings taken by force, but not in the case of South Sakhalin and the southern Kuriles, which Japan had obtained from czarist Russia in the course of legally concluded and internationally binding treaties. Finally, with reference to Korea, the Japanese colony in due course was to become free and independent. The Cairo Declaration meant to turn the clock back to pre-Perry times as far as Japanese territory was involved. In February 1945, at Yalta, in order to gain Soviet support of the projected invasion of the Japanese homeland later that year, Roosevelt promised to restore to the Soviet Union pre-1904 Russian rights in Manchuria, and gave to it titles to the Kuriles and to South Sakhalin.

Japan Faces Defeat

By 1945, with tightened submarine warfare and air raids against the home islands themselves, the war had definitely turned against Japan. Japanese merchant ships had difficulty getting raw materials and importing food. Manpower was shifted from agriculture to military needs. The war effort was adversely affected by hasty reallocations of human resources. After the conclusion of the war in Europe, Harry S Truman, the new American president who took over after Roosevelt's death in April 1945; Clement Attlee, who had succeeded Churchill as the British prime minister; and Marshal Stalin reiterated the Yalta agreements at Potsdam. They outlined the zones of occupation in Asia. The Americans were to receive the Japanese surrenders in Japan, the Philippines, the Pacific islands, and Korea south of the 38th parallel; the Soviets, in northern Japanese islands, North Korea, and Manchuria; the Chinese under Chiang Kai-shek, in China and Indochina to the 15th parallel; and the British, in Southeast Asia. The Potsdam Declaration called for the elimination of militarism in Japan, the occupation of Japan, and the territorial limitations of Japan to its four main islands and adjacent minor ones.

The terms of the Potsdam Declaration were relayed to Tokyo, where, in the ensuing weeks, debates raged around the emperor as to their acceptance or rejection. The conclusion of the war was hastened by three factors: the atomic bombs dropped on Hiroshima and Nagasaki on August 6 and 9, respectively, and the entrance of the Soviet Union (which prematurely scrapped the five-year 1941 neutrality treaty) into the Pacific war on August 8. The Japanese, despite last-ditch opposition from the army, followed an imperial rescript on August 15 (Victory in Japan or V-J Day) to lay down their arms. Two weeks after the call for capitulation, on Sunday, September 2, 1945, the instrument of surrender was signed on the U.S. battleship *Missouri*, in Tokyo Bay. It was signed by representatives of the military and foreign office in Tokyo, General MacArthur on behalf of all the Allies, and a battery of signers from individual participating countries in the Pacific war. As stipulated in the Potsdam Declaration, additional surrenders were concluded in other countries. In the holocaust over the years 1937 to 1945, 3.1 million Japanese had lost their lives: 2.3 million soldiers died on the various fronts; 300,000 civilians were overseas casualties; and 500,000 others, including atomic bomb victims in Japan, perished. Casualties of other involved nationalities totaled into unnumbered tens of millions of lives.

Japan was defeated, militarism was eradicated, and, for the first time in modern Asian history, there appeared the spectacle of a weak, occupied Japan.

The Atomic Bombings: A Look Back

BY JOHN W. DOWER

Facing up to questionable acts committed during World War II seems to be difficult for nations to do. Among the combatants, only Germany has thoroughly and publicly accepted responsibility for horrific acts. In Japan, recollections of the war are largely suppressed, distorted, or disregarded. In the United States, discussion of World War II has been far more open, but as the victors, Americans tend to cast themselves in heroic roles. Without a doubt, there was much American heroism and sacrifice during World War II. Yet questions linger over the use of atomic bombs to obliterate Hiroshima and Nagasaki in the war's closing days. In the following essay, historian John W. Dower discusses the legacy of the bombings, including differing views in Japan and America on whether the bombings were necessary or justified.

Fiftieth anniversaries of historical events—particularly wars—breed controversy. The emotion-laden memories of survivors from the events of a half-century ago collide with the skepticism and detachment of younger generations. Historians with access to previously inaccessible (or ignored) material offer new perspectives. Politicians milk the still palpable human connection between past and present for every possible drop of ideological elixir.

The fiftieth anniversary of the end of World War II in Asia has become especially contentious. Why is this so, when presumably we are commemorating victory over an enemy generally regarded as aggressive, atrocious, and fanatical? The answer, of course, is that defeating Japan ultimately entailed incinerating and

John W. Dower, "Hiroshima, Nagasaki, and the Politics of Memory," *Technology Review*, vol. 98, August/September 1995, pp. 48–51. Copyright © 1995 by the Association of Alumni and Alumnae of MIT. Reproduced by permission.

irradiating tens of thousands of men, women, and children with a weapon more terrible than any previously known or imagined.

Unfortunately, Americans have been denied a rare opportunity to use the fiftieth anniversary of Hiroshima and Nagasaki to reflect more deeply about these world-changing developments. This opportunity was lost early this year [1995] when the Smithsonian Institution, bowing to political pressure, agreed to drastically scale back a proposed exhibit at the National Air and Space Museum in Washington depicting the development of the atomic bombs and their use against Japan.

As initially envisioned by the Smithsonian's curators, the exhibition would have taken viewers through a succession of rooms that introduced, in turn, the ferocity of the last year of the war in Asia, the development of the bomb, the unfolding imperatives behind the U.S. decision to use the weapon against Japan, preparation for the *Enola Gay* mission that dropped the first bomb on Hiroshima (with the fuselage of the *Enola Gay* itself being the centerpiece of the exhibition), the human consequences of the bombs in the two target cities, and the nuclear legacy to the postwar world. Occasional placards were to have summarized controversies that have emerged in scholarship and public discourse on these matters over the past decades.

This ambitious proposed exhibit proved to be politically unacceptable. The Senate unanimously denounced the original draft script as being "revisionist and offensive to many World War II veterans." It was grossly misleading and morally obtuse, the critics declared, to focus the exhibit so intensely on questions about the bombs, and on the Japanese suffering in Hiroshima and Nagasaki, without comparable portrayal of Japanese atrocities that extended from Nanking to Pearl Harbor to Bataan to Manila. The chief historian of the Air Force (who had privately praised the original draft) asked publicly how the Smithsonian had managed to make a hash of such a "morally unambiguous" subject as the use of the bombs.

Museum Caves In

Confronted by such criticism, the Smithsonian—like Japan 50 years earlier—surrendered unconditionally. Visitors to the Air and Space Museum will encounter a small exhibition featuring the fuselage of the *Enola Gay* and a brief tape and text explaining that this was the plane that dropped the first atomic bomb, following which, nine days later, Japan surrendered. The artifact, it is now argued, speaks for itself.

Artifacts do not speak for themselves, and the decision to scrap original plans for an ambitious and nuanced exhibition represents the triumph of patriotic orthodoxy over serious historical reflection and reconstruction. No one denies that the Smithsonian's original script had problems and needed revisions (the curators themselves readily circulated their first draft for critical comments). The benign and minimalist exhibit we have ended up with, however, is a travesty—an appallingly simplistic and nationalistic way of representing one of the most momentous and destructive developments of the twentieth century. Instead of using the fiftieth anniversary of Hiroshima and Nagasaki to reflect on the confluence of triumph and tragedy that occurred in August 1945, we have turned this into another occasion to perpetuate a heroic national myth.

The orthodox account argues that the war in Asia was a brutal struggle against a fanatical, expansionist foe (which is true, albeit cavalier about European and American colonial control in Asia up to 1941). This righteous war against Japanese aggression was ended, the heroic narrative continues, by the dropping of the atomic bombs, which saved enormous numbers of American lives that otherwise would have been sacrificed in the invasion of Japan that was deemed necessary to force a surrender. As the Senate's condemnation of the Smithsonian's plans put it, the atomic bombs brought the war to a "merciful" end.

President Truman and his advisers clearly did consider the bombs as a way of hastening the war's end and saving American lives. Few historians, however, now regard this as the only motivation behind the decision. Facts that complicate the orthodox narrative, for example, include the Soviet entry into the war against Japan on August 8, 1945, two days after Hiroshima. Most Japanese accounts then and since weigh the Soviet declaration of war as being at least as shocking as the Hiroshima bombing to the Japanese leadership. The United States had long solicited Soviet entry into the war against Japan, and knew it was imminent. Why the haste to drop the bomb before the effect of the Soviet declaration of war could be measured?

The heroic narrative similarly fails to question the need for the atomic bombing of Nagasaki on August 9, which occurred before Japan's high command had a chance to assess Hiroshima and the Soviet entry. Indeed, even many Japanese who now accept that Hiroshima may have been necessary to crack the no-surrender policy of Japanese militarists maintain that Nagasaki was plainly and simply a war crime.

Also generally neglected in the heroic narrative is that the United States was not on the brink of invading Japan in August of 1945. The preliminary assault, aimed at the southern island of Kyushu, was slated for no earlier than November 1, and the invasion of Tokyo and the Kanto area on the main island of Honshu would not have commenced until March 1946. There was time to consider options. Other information suggests that an invasion may not have been necessary at all. A famous report by the U.S. Strategic Bombing Survey, published in 1946, concluded that Japan was so materially and psychologically weakened by August 1945 that it would have been forced to surrender by year's end, and probably by November 1—without the atomic bombs, without the Soviet entry, and without an invasion.

Alternatives to using the atomic bombs on civilian targets also became known after Japan's surrender. Navy planners, for example, believed that intensified economic strangulation would bring Japan to its knees; the country's merchant marine had been sunk by 1945. Within the Manhattan Project, the possibility of dropping the bomb on a "demonstration" target, with Japanese observers present, had been broached but rejected—partly for fear that the demonstration bomb might be a dud and would lead the Japanese to fight even more ferociously. Conservative officials such as Undersecretary of State Joseph Grew, the former ambassador to Japan, argued that the Japanese could be persuaded to surrender if the United States abandoned its policy of demanding unconditional surrender and guaranteed that the emperor would be allowed to keep his throne. Through their code-breaking operations, the Americans also were aware that, beginning in mid-June, the Japanese had made vague overtures to the Soviet Union concerning negotiating an end to the war.

Japan: An Early Target

While it was fear of a Nazi bomb that originally propelled the Manhattan Project, it now is known that U.S. planners had identified Japan as the prime target for the atomic bomb as early as 1943—a year or more before it became clear that Germany was not attempting to build such a weapon. One reason for this shift of target was the fear that if the bomb didn't work, sophisticated German scientists and engineers might be able to disassemble it and figure out how to build their own. (No one worried that the Japanese had this capability.)

The development and deployment of the bombs also became driven by almost irresistible technological and scientific imperatives. J. Robert Oppenheimer spoke for many of his brilliant colleagues on the Manhattan Project when he later acknowledged how "technically sweet" the enterprise had been. Oppenheimer also confided that after Germany's surrender on May 8, 1945, he and his fellow scientists intensified their efforts out of concern that the war might end before they could finish. Secretary of War Henry Stimson, the elder statesman who took deep pride in his moralism, observed at one point that it was essential to try the new weapon out on a real target. The original justification for moving to a new order of destructive weaponry had evaporated, and the weaponry itself had begun to create its own rationale.

Sheer visceral hatred abetted the targeting of Japan for nuclear destruction. Although many critics of the Smithsonian's original plans took umbrage at a statement calling attention to the element of vengeance in the American war against Japan, few historians (or honest participants) would discount that this was a factor. Japan had, after all, attacked the United States. "Remember Pearl Harbor—Keep 'em Dying" was a popular military slogan from the outset of the war, and among commentators and war correspondents at the time it was a commonplace that the racially and culturally alien Japanese were vastly more despised than their German allies.

U.S. leaders also had postwar politics on their minds—both global and domestic. Documents declassified since the 1960s make unmistakably clear that from the spring of 1945, top-level policymakers hoped that the bomb would dissuade Stalin from pursuing Soviet expansion into Eastern Europe and elsewhere. Some individuals closely involved with the development of the bomb (such as Arthur Compton, Edward Teller, and James Conant) further argued that the new weapon's very horrendousness compelled its use against a real city, so that the postwar world would understand the need to cooperate on arms control. At the same time, shrewd readers of the domestic political winds in the United States warned that if the Manhattan Project ended with nothing dramatic to show for its efforts, the postwar Congress surely would launch a hostile investigation into the huge disbursal of secret funds.

Decades of Suffering

The Japanese now estimate that within months of the attacks, around 140,000 people probably died in Hiroshima and 70,000 in Nagasaki. That is about double the figures typically reported in Western accounts, which are based on U.S. calculations made shortly after the bombs were dropped.

Such figures fail to take into account the peculiar long-term legacies of nuclear devastation. Because of the uncertain genetic effects of radiation poisoning, for example, hibakusha, as the atomic bomb survivors are known, became undesirable marriage prospects. And although no genetic harm to succeeding generations has been identified, irradiated survivors and their progeny have lived with gnawing fear that the curse of the bombs may be transgenerational. In the Japanese idiom, many survivors suffer "keloids of the heart" and "leukemia of the spirit."

More concretely, Japanese continue to die of atomic-bomb related diseases. Survivors suffer higher-than-normal rates of leukemia and cancers of the thyroid, breast, lung, stomach, and salivary glands. The Japanese government now estimates total nuclear fatalities in the two cities—including belated deaths that can be traced to the bombs—at between 300,000 and 350,000. (Total U.S. combat deaths in the Pacific War numbered slightly less than 100,000.) Moreover, infants exposed to radiation in utero before the eighteenth week who were born mentally retarded now are 50-year-old retarded adults, many with elderly parents who agonize over what will become of these microcephalic "pika babies" after the parents die.

Another fact commonly neglected in the orthodox American treatment of the bomb is that thousands of the victims were not Japanese. According to Japanese estimates, between 6,500 and 10,000 Koreans were killed in Hiroshima and Nagasaki; Koreans themselves put the number even higher. (Most of these Koreans were colonial subjects of Japan who had been conscripted for heavy labor.) The bomb also killed more than 1,000 second-generation Japanese-Americans who had been temporarily living in Hiroshima when the Japanese attacked Pearl Harbor in 1941 and whom the war had prevented from returning to the United States. Several hundred Chinese likely died in the nuclear blasts as well, along with small numbers of Southeast Asian students, British and Dutch POWs [prisoners of war], and European priests. About two dozen Caucasian-American POWs survived the atomic bombing of Hiroshima, only to be beaten to death by Japanese hibakusha.

The Japanese Perspective

In Japan, as might be expected, popular memory of the atomic bombs tends to begin where the conventional American narrative leaves off—with what took place beneath the mushroom clouds of Hiroshima and Nagasaki. The Japanese dwell on the extraordinary human misery the bombs caused, providing intimate stories about the shattering of individual lives. Oe Kenzaburo, the 1994 Nobel laureate in literature, called attention to this in a series of influential essays written in the early 1960s. In Oe's rendering, the hibakusha were "moralists," for they had experienced "the cruelest days in human history" and never lost "the vision of a nation that will do its best to materialize a world without any nuclear weapons."

This perception of the significance of Hiroshima and Nagasaki—starkly different from that conveyed in the triumphal American narrative—clearly has the potential to become myopic and nationalistic. Japan risks turning the attacks on Hiroshima and Nagasaki into a "victimization" narrative, in which the bombs fell from the heavens without context—as if war began on August 6, 1945, and ended on August 9, and innocent Japan bore the cross of witnessing the horror of the new nuclear age. But Oe's account, like most other popular Japanese discourse on these matters, is more subtle than this. Since the early 1970s the Japanese media have devoted much attention to the thesis that "victims" can simultaneously be the victimizers of others—as the hibakusha in Hiroshima demonstrated when they beat to death American POWs.

It is virtually a cliché in the U.S. media that the Japanese suffer from historical amnesia and are incapable of honestly confronting their World War II past. There is much truth to this. For many years, Japanese textbooks presented a sanitized version of the conflict. Schoolchildren were taught that Japan "advanced" into China, rather than "invaded" its neighbor. Doubt was cast on the reality of the Rape of Nanking. Japan's colonial repression of other Asians was barely mentioned. To the present day, conservative politicians have refused to support a clear and un-equivocal official statement acknowledging Japan's acts of aggression and atrocity and forthrightly apologizing for them. At the same time, however, domestic debate on these matters has been far more intense than the foreign media usually acknowledges. In recent years—especially since the death of Emperor Hirohito in 1989—the textbooks have become more forthright, while the Japanese national media have carried detailed commentary on virtually all aspects of Japan's war behavior. In this context, certainly in light of the fiasco at the Smithsonian, it is anomalous for Americans to be accusing others of sanitizing the past and suffering from historical amnesia.

All Sides Targeted Civilians

In the end, one of the great legacies of World War II was the redefinition of the legitimate targets of war to include noncombatant women, children, and men. Japan itself was one of the first countries to act out this new view of war; its bombing of Chinese cities in 1937 was passionately condemned by the League of Nations and the United States as behavior beyond the pale of civilized people. Picasso's great mural of the bombing of Guernica in the same year by the fascists during the Spanish civil war evoked the shock that similar barbarity aroused.

By the end of World War II, however, even the democratic nations had accepted the targeting of civilian populations as proper and inevitable. Earlier in 1945, British and U.S. air forces obliterated much of Dresden after previously fire-bombing other German cities. In Japan, U.S. saturation bombing devastated Tokyo and 63 other cities, killing around 100,000 civilians in Tokyo alone. The atomic bombs were simply a more efficient way of terrorizing enemies and destroying a newly legitimized target of war: civilian morale.

In the fires of Hiroshima and Nagasaki, triumph and tragedy became inseparable. At the same time, America's victory became fused with a future of inescapable insecurity. The bombs marked both an end and a beginning. They marked the end of an appalling global conflagration that killed more than 55 million people and the beginning of the nuclear arms race—and a world in which security was forever a step away.

THE HISTORY OF NATIONS
Chapter 5

The Postwar Era

The Occupation

By Richard Storry

In Japan's recorded history, no invader had ever defeated the nation. Most famously, the Mongol fleets of Kublai Khan were twice crippled by great storms during attempted invasions of Japan in 1274 and 1281. These seemingly miraculous "kamikaze" or "divine winds," contributed to the national myth of invincibility. Most Japanese were, therefore, stunned when their emperor, in a recorded broadcast on August 15, 1945, called on them to "bear the unbearable" and peacefully accept unconditional surrender. Many expected the worst when the U.S.-led occupation of Japan began two weeks later. Indeed, some Japanese committed suicide to avoid life under foreign rule. As Oxford historian Richard Storry recounts, however, the vast majority of Japanese were simply relieved to see the war come to an end and were pleasantly surprised at the relatively benign and progressive occupation that followed.

It was at the end of August [1945] that the vanguard of the American army of occupation landed at an airfield near Tokyo. They were driven in Japanese transport to Yokohama, which was to be the headquarters of General Eichelberger's Eighth Army. As they entered what was left of the city they observed few spectators among the ruins. At every intersection stood a Japanese soldier, rifle and bayonet at the ready, with his back to the convoy. This was a precaution against any possible attack or demonstration. On the whole it was a dismal scene, suggestive of little triumph for the victors. The desolation was heightened, if anything, by the fact that the electric trains were still running along the embankment on the main line to Tokyo.

After the emperor's broadcast all kinds of rumors about the Americans had begun to spread among the people. There was a general belief that the occupying troops, filled with vengeful hatred of the Japanese, would be virtually unrestrained in their behaviour towards life and property. Many people—women especially—thought it prudent to leave Tokyo and Yokohama before the Americans moved in. But as the troops arrived by air and sea, it was soon evident that popular fears were groundless. The Americans did not behave like demons at all. So began perhaps the most peaceful and, to outward appearance, most harmonious occupation of one great country by another that has ever been known.

First Defeat

Japan had never known defeat, much less occupation. The people, then, had really no idea as to how they should conduct themselves in a situation that lacked all precedent. Moreover, they were confused, dazed, weary, and a quarter starved. Most of them were too relieved that the war was over to cherish much resentment against those who had defeated them, especially when the enemy turned out to be far less vindictive than had been feared. Popular resentment, in so far as it existed at all, was directed against the national leaders, in particular the generals and admirals who had led Japan into a hopeless war. Such men, it was felt, had betrayed both the emperor and the people of Japan. Towards the Americans, once the sense of unreasoning fear had been dispelled, the dominant feeling was one of friendly curiosity. . . .

The formal ceremony of surrender took place on 2 September 1945, on the deck of the American battleship *Missouri*, in the presence of the man who was to take charge of the Occupation, General MacArthur, Supreme Commander for the Allied Powers. The abbreviation of this title, SCAP, came to stand both for the man himself and for his headquarters in Tokyo, and it is so used by historians. It is perhaps too early to offer a fair assessment of MacArthur as Supreme Commander in Japan from September 1945 to April 1951, when he was dismissed by President Truman. But some things can be said with assurance, by way of an interim judgement. MacArthur revealed himself as that rare figure, the American version of the traditional British grandee. . . .

Swift Reform

In a remarkably short time the battered apparatus of Japan's war machine was dismantled or destroyed. The repatriation from overseas of some three million Japanese, civilians as well as soldiers and sailors, was successfully organized and completed. When starvation seemed to be a real threat, towards the end of 1945, SCAP took action to import foodstuffs from the United States, and these imports were continued for the next few years. Retribution, in the form of trials and purges, was visited on the unjust and, so far as the purges were concerned, sometimes also on the just. SCAP was responsible for a new code covering labour relations, whereby all manner of old abuses were swept away, on paper at any rate. SCAP wrote a new Constitution for Japan and directed the Japanese government to recast the judicial and administrative structure throughout the country. An ambitious programme of land reform was introduced. The *zaibatsu* [business conglomerates] were dissolved; the Home Ministry was abolished; political prisoners, some of whom had spent seventeen years in gaol [jail], were released. The watchwords were democracy and decentralization. . . .

In the first phase of the Occupation, from September 1945 to about the end of 1947, Japan experienced the full force of a bloodless social and cultural revolution inspired and supervised by General Headquarters, SCAP. It is important to bear in mind, however, that the Japanese people on the whole welcomed many of the reforms introduced by the government on instructions from SCAP. Once the war was over and the almost intolerable pressure of the police state was removed, all kinds of forces, dammed up for years, were suddenly released.

It was in October 1945 that the government was instructed to set free political prisoners; and out of gaol came a small band of dedicated Communists, some of whom had been behind bars for years. Unchecked by the police, they began to organize a new Japanese Communist Party, and in the acute economic distress and social confusion of the immediate post-war period they made much headway. But the Communists formed only a part of a resurgent left-wing movement, reflecting popular dissatisfaction with almost every established institution. The army, for example, was completely discredited. Repatriated soldiers found a Japan that no longer cared for them. They had left their homes as heroes. They returned as living ghosts, to be submerged in the anonymous masses struggling for a bare livelihood.

The farmers, however, were somewhat better off than in the past. For inflation wiped out debts, and the countryside swarmed with visitors from the cities and towns in search of food to supplement the inadequate basic rations authorized by the government. Every evening the trains returned to the cities bulging with foragers. These trains symbolized the misery and confusion that prevailed for many months after the Surrender. When they were

overcrowded to the point of suffocation there still were some energetic people who contrived to climb into the carriages through
the open windows. Others rode on the buffers of the locomotive and on the couplings between the coaches. Everyone had
with him a large bundle or rucksack. On the outward journey
this contained household possessions which, it was hoped, could
be exchanged for rice or vegetables. On the return journey there
was always the risk of a police raid, followed by confiscation of
the black market food. For city dwellers the winter of 1945–6
was very grim indeed. . . .

No Longer Divine

The *mystique* surrounding the emperor was soon dissipated, in
part as a result of pressure from SCAP and in part by the emperor's
own wish. He was willing to abdicate in favour of his elder son,
for he felt acutely that he should accept responsibility for the war.
Moreover, an entirely new era had begun with the Occupation,
and it seemed fitting therefore that Japan should make a new start
under a new emperor. Abdication, or retirement, had taken place
on a great many occasions in the past without affecting the prestige of the imperial house. But in 1945 his advisers urged that
the emperor at least defer any intention to abdicate, because they
feared for the monarchy's very survival should the emperor retire, for this would imply that the fortunes of the imperial house
were indissolubly linked with those of the now generally despised
Supreme Command. Furthermore it would be easier for the victorious Allies to indict an ex-emperor as a war criminal than to
take action against a reigning monarch. All the same, when the
emperor called on General MacArthur not long after the Surrender he declared that he himself, rather than any of his generals and ministers, should be held responsible for the war. It was
on this occasion that a celebrated photograph was taken—and,
on SCAP instructions, given much publicity—of the emperor and
MacArthur standing side by side. The former, in a morning coat
and striped trousers, was shown standing stiffly beside the much
taller American, who looked quite relaxed and informal in his
open-necked shirt, with his hands resting in his belt straps. At the
time most foreigners and some Japanese believed that this photograph would do immense damage to the personal prestige of
the emperor, who at first sight looked indeed not at all impressive beside his conqueror. Nearly all previous photographs of the

emperor had shown him in uniform; and the one that had made perhaps the most powerful mass impact had been the annual photograph, reproduced in newsfilms all over the country, of the

HARD TIMES FOR ORDINARY JAPANESE

Amid shortages of housing, food, and fuel, life continued to be bitterly hard for ordinary Japanese even after the war. Mutsuo Saito, then a young man just out of uniform, recalls conditions in the only place his family could find to rent a room in 1946—the brothel district of Tokyo.

Food was very scarce then. For a while my parents went off to Yamagata, because they knew that, being farther away from Tokyo, there would be fewer shortages there, and father thought that some of his relatives or friends might be able to sell him rice. When my parents found rice to buy, they wrote to me to come and collect it. Then I would go and buy a black-market railway ticket and go to Yamagata to fetch the rice. You had to buy black-market tickets, because for ordinary tickets you needed to queue for days. The black marketeers would get waifs and strays to sit in the queue for them, and then they would sell the tickets at some vastly inflated price.

When I wasn't fetching rice from Yamagata, I had nothing to do at all. I didn't even bother to get up in the morning. When we woke up, the lodger and I would take out a *shōgi* [Japanese chess] board which we had, and lie in our eiderdowns on the matted floor playing *shōgi* until it was time to go to sleep again.

White rice was so precious in those days that, when my parents came back, we decided that we wouldn't eat the rice right away. We would keep it for special occasions. The rest of the time we lived on sweet potatoes, which were relatively plentiful around Honjō even then.

Tessa Morris-Suzuki, *Showa: An Inside History of Hirohito's Japan.* London: The Athlone Press, 1984.

New Year parade in Tokyo, showing the emperor in a field-marshal's uniform mounted on a pure white horse. But if the old respect was diminished by the photograph taken at MacArthur's headquarters in 1945, a feeling of sympathy was greatly strengthened; and on reflection many Japanese came to believe that the emperor, in this rather pathetic post-war photograph, showed a certain unassailable dignity. In January 1946 the emperor issued a rescript formally renouncing any claims to a divine or semi-divine status, and to reinforce his wish to be regarded by everyone solely as a human being he undertook a number of unprecedented informal tours of the land. As the Japanese put it, 'he came down from the clouds'. Often surrounded by foreign news cameramen, or even by coloured [black] American M.P.s, he appeared in an altogether new role, that of a tired, middle-aged man in rather old civilian clothes. He talked, in a somewhat halting way, to people in the fields, or at the work bench, or in hospital. For all to see he was a very human, bookish, rather shy, sincere man in his forties. . . .

War Crimes Trials

Eventually an international tribunal, on the Nuremburg pattern, sat for some two years and at the end passed sentence of death on seven Japanese leaders, including two former Prime Ministers, Tojo and Hirota. Eighteen others were sentenced to various terms of imprisonment. The voluminous documentation accompanying the International Military Tribunal for the Far East has been of great interest to historians, but it cannot be said that the Tokyo Trial made a deep impression upon the Japanese. They accepted it as the possibly inevitable punishment meted out by the victors upon the vanquished. Tojo, whose stock was very low after a bungled attempt to kill himself, somewhat enhanced his reputation by accepting, in court, full responsibility for starting the Pacific War. People felt sorry for Tojo and the others in the dock, but they did not make martyrs or heroes of them. On the whole the Japanese reaction to the Tokyo Trial was one of boredom. . . .

New Constitution

Probably the most important action taken by scap in the first year of the Occupation was the preparation of a new Constitution for Japan. The government had been told that the existing Constitution would have to be amended very radically and that this ought to be done as quickly as possible. Accordingly the Shidehara cabinet appointed a committee to draft the necessary revisions; but its suggestions did not satisfy General Headquarters. They did not go far enough, in the opinion of SCAP, towards removing the undemocratic principles expressed and implied in the Meiji Constitution. So MacArthur's own staff produced a document, in effect an entirely new Constitution, and this was presented to the cabinet with the verbal ultimatum that if it was rejected the Supreme Commander would place the draft before the Japanese people, in advance of the first post-war general election planned for the spring of 1946.

When the members of MacArthur's Government Section set about the task of drafting the Constitution they were given, by way of guidance, three principles on which the document was to be based. In the first place the monarchy should be retained, but it must be subject to the will of the people. Secondly, war was to be foresworn for ever. Thirdly, 'all forms of feudalism' must be abolished. The resultant document was adopted by the Diet with only minor alterations and was promulgated as the new Constitution in October 1946. It stated that sovereignty rested not with

Japanese soldiers in Okinawa surrender to Allied forces.

the emperor but with the people of Japan; and the Diet became 'the highest organ of the state'. The emperor was defined as a symbol of the state and of the unity of the people. It was this section of the draft Constitution that attracted the most critical attention during the debates in the Diet. The cabinet minister charged with the duty of presenting the Constitution to the two Houses went to ingenious lengths to explain that the drastic change in the emperor's status did not impair Japan's *kokutai*, or basic national polity. Nevertheless, the notion of the sovereignty of the people was revolutionary in Japanese eyes; and many constitutional lawyers have argued that this principle, together with the description of the Diet as the supreme organ of the state, means that Japan is a republic in fact if not in name. Ambassadors, for example, are now appointed not by the emperor but by the cabinet....

Japan's New Leader

A single Japanese politician dominated the scene during the Occupation and for two years thereafter. This was Yoshida Shigeru. Succeeding Shidehara as Premier in the spring of 1946, he held office until a year later, when what proved to be a temporary swing to the Left gave the Socialists, under Katayama, a numerical lead in the General Election of April 1947. Katayama was followed by Ashida, who was in office only eight months, until October 1948. In this month Yoshida formed his second cabinet. He won a general election in January 1949. He was to be victorious in three more elections before his resignation in November 1954. In all he was Prime Minister five times and held office for nearly seven years. A former ambassador in London, Yoshida's life had been spent in the foreign service, and he was nearly seventy when he became Premier for the first time. He was untouched by the purge—which eliminated, for some years, his chief political rival, Hatoyama—because he had been arrested by the *Kempei* [national security police] in 1945 for advocating an early peace. For this reason he was *persona grata* with the Occupation authorities in their earlier, reforming, phase. Later he was equally acceptable as a staunch Conservative. At the same time the Japanese admired him as one who combined obedience to SCAP directives with a certain evident, though not readily definable, independence of manner. It was part of his *panache* to assume a rather English air, suggested by his choice of clothes and his attachment to a well-worn Rolls-Royce, reputedly the only one in Tokyo. This, it was thought, was a mild, calculated irritation to the dominant Americans. Such trivialities counted for the Japanese in the first years of the Occupation and made Yoshida popular. After the Peace Treaty came into force this popularity dwindled away and he seemed, in Japanese eyes, to be no more than a very obstinate, cantankerous, dictatorial old man. At all events Yoshida symbolized something indestructible in Japanese life; and as this, whatever it was, clearly excluded any sympathy with Communism, it was welcomed by the Americans. Considering what was happening in China, they regarded a moderately right-wing Japan as an international asset.

Aided by Korean War

The outbreak of the Korean War in the summer of 1950 naturally confirmed the Americans in this opinion. There was a moment, early in the war, when South Korea was nearly lost. Had the Americans been faced at the same time with the problem of an unreliable, restive Japan, their difficulties would have been formidable indeed. But Japan was a firm base from which support could be given to South Korea. In fact MacArthur was able at one stage to denude Japan of troops without any real anxiety. The Japanese, for their part, did well out of the war. So-called 'special procurements' for the United Nations' forces gave a great fillip to Japan's economic revival, which had just started in a modest way, thanks to a programme of wage and price stability introduced at the beginning of 1949 in response to pressure from SCAP. By 1950 the shattered cities were almost, if not quite completely, rebuilt in a rough-and-ready sort of way. Once the Korean War was in its stride Japanese factories and workshops were busy manufacturing the multitudinous variety of supplies required by the fighting services in Korea. As the war continued for some three years, the boom was very considerable. By the end of 1951 Japanese industrial production was roughly equal to what it had been twenty years previously.

As conditions improved and national morale recovered, the Occupation, although never very frankly opposed except by the Communists, became increasingly irksome in Japanese eyes. When MacArthur was summarily dismissed by President Truman in April 1951, the Japanese received the news with genuine astonishment. Their first thought was that this might in some way adversely affect the discussions already begun between the Yoshida cabinet and the President's special adviser John Foster Dulles, on a treaty of peace. This anxiety was mingled with the real sadness felt by the Japanese when they bowed farewell to the remarkable egotist who had governed them with some success for the past five and a half years. But the President lost little time in issuing a statement saying that Dulles would shortly revisit Japan for further talks.

Indeed the preparation of the Japanese Peace Treaty—signed on 8 September 1951 at San Francisco—was very largely in the hands of the indefatigable Dulles, who made several visits to Japan and who also contrived to win the agreement of Great Britain, Australia, and other countries to the kind of settlement he envisaged, namely one that would be free of punitive and restrictive features of any kind....

Peace Treaty Signed

In the end, having obtained the agreement of the great majority of the governments concerned, the United States felt ready to summon what was only in name a peace conference. It was, rather, a formal gathering to endorse what had already been decided. The invitation to San Francisco was issued jointly by the United States and Great Britain to Japan and to the nations that had fought against her; but neither Communist nor Nationalist China was invited.

Prime Minister Yoshida, as chief delegate, signed the Treaty of Peace for Japan. Forty-eight other nations signed the document. The Soviet delegate, Gromyko, made a strongly worded speech attacking the Treaty. As was expected, his country, together with Poland and Czechoslovakia, refused to sign it.

By the terms of the San Francisco Treaty Japan recognized the independence of Korea and renounced all claims to Formosa and the Pescadores, to south Sakhalin and the Kuriles, and to the former mandated islands in the Pacific. American control for the time being of the Ryukyu and Bonin Islands was accepted. Such was the formal liquidation of an empire gained and lost in the course of eighty years. The Treaty placed no limitations on Japanese economy and trade; and Japan's right to self-defence, in accordance with the principles of the United Nations' Charter, was recognized.

On the same day that the San Francisco Treaty was signed—

8 September 1951—the United States concluded with Japan a security pact in which Japan requested the retention of American forces in and about her territory as a defence against attack from overseas. In the pact the United States expressed the belief that Japan would 'increasingly assume responsibility for its own defence . . . always avoiding any armament which would be an offensive threat'.

The Treaty came into force on 28 April 1952; and on that date, the eve of the emperor's birthday, the Occupation officially ceased and Japan was once again formally an independent nation.

Economic Superpower

By Martin E. Weinstein

After sputtering during the 1950s, and relying largely on U.S. relief aid and military supply orders for growth, Japan's economy leaped onto the world stage in the 1960s. Observers were astounded by its sustained double-digit growth and the rising quality, diversity, and sophistication of its export goods. Terms like "economic superpower" and "miracle economy" began to be applied to Japan, and more than one commentator predicted that by the end of the century, Japan's economy would be the largest in the world. In this selection, written just after that phenomenal decade, political scientist Martin E. Weinstein explores the causes of Japan's economic rebound from the devastation of World War II.

Between 1950 and 1960, Japan's economic growth rate averaged better than 10 percent a year. From 1960 to 1970, it was a little less than 12 percent a year, causing Japan's production of goods and services to quadruple during the decade. Japan now has the third largest and by far the fastest growing developed economy in the world.

The visible contrast between Japan and its Asian neighbors makes clear the distinction between developed and developing economies. Communist China and India are in the throes of industrialization, but together with most other states in the region they remain predominantly rural. Literacy in these countries is slowly increasing, but most of the people's horizons are still bounded by their villages. Except in a few major cities, good roads are scarce and motor vehicles, even scarcer. Refrigerators and television sets are luxuries enjoyed by only the wealthy few. To an urbanized American or European, most of Asia is rural and poor. If not always peaceful and secure, life is relatively simple.

Martin E. Weinstein, "The Phenomenal Economy," *Japan: Asian Power*, edited by Irwin Isenberg. New York: H.W. Wilson, 1971, pp. 73-80. Copyright © 1971 by The H.W. Wilson Company. Reproduced by permission.

Sudden Prosperity

Japan presents a dramatic contrast. The number of Japanese engaged in the primary sector—farming, fishing and forestry—has dropped from a relatively low 37 percent in 1955, to less than 20 percent today. More than 60 percent of the people live in cities of 50,000 or more. Tokyo, with over 10 million people, is the most populous metropolis in the world. Every Japanese city is clogged with cars, trucks and buses made in Japan. The highways and superhighways which are beginning to connect the major urban centers are heavily used. Business offices and factories operate in large, modern ferroconcrete and glass buildings. Most people still live in quarters that are cramped and ill-heated by American standards. But virtually every household is equipped with a refrigerator, a washing machine and a TV—increasingly, a color TV. The trains and buses are packed with well-dressed commuters and shoppers, carrying the newspapers, journals and books that make Japan the most literate country in the world. The mass media provide a constant bombardment of advertising. In the numerous coffee shops, juke boxes play the latest rock music or Beethoven. Over this thriving, noisy, industrialized urban Japan, hangs a pall of dust, smoke and smog.

Japan's phenomenal prosperity and economic growth rate raise a number of basic questions. First, what is the explanation for Japan's economic performance? Second, what are the implications of Japan's economic record for the developing countries of non-European origin? Can Japan serve as a model for them? Third, what are the prospects for Japan's future economic growth?

The Meiji Legacy

In trying to understand Japan's economic development and current growth rate, it is most important to remember when this surge began. Japan's industrialization . . . had its origins not in the twentieth century of rising expectations, but in the nineteenth century, when poverty and social injustice were commonly accepted as the human condition. Japan's population in 1870, when the Meiji leaders were coming to power, was 33 million. Although they were predominantly an agricultural, rural society, the Japanese even then had a literacy rate of about 30 per cent, much higher than most of Asia, Africa or Latin America today. Moreover, the people had been indoctrinated for centuries in the virtues of diligence, thrift and loyal obedience to feudal lords and village heads. The ruling, quasi-military class, or *samurai*, had a strong tradition of honesty, selfless devotion to duty and a healthy respect for individual merit. In the 1870s and 1880s, the Meiji leaders themselves were mostly young, lower-ranking samurai, whose intelligence, energy and courage brought them to the fore when Japan was threatened by Western encroachment. Moreover, the values of Japanese society were secular—here and now—rather than otherworldly. They were relatively well prepared to industrialize. Economic historians have noted that many elements of the Protestant ethic, which, some historians believe motivated Europe's industrialization, were present in mid-nineteenth century Japan. The Meiji leaders employed these human resources with great skill and patience. They planned and worked at industrialization for the entire forty years of their political supremacy—from the 1870s to World War I. They introduced Western education and technology in a highly pragmatic and selective way, aiming at steady growth and minimal social dislocation, rather than spectacular economic leaps. They encouraged entrepreneurs and capitalists, but they did not idealize laissez-faire capitalism as a doctrine. On the contrary, the Meiji government practiced close bureaucratic supervision and regulation of banking and industry, as the Japanese government still does today. Thrift, low wages and careful management assured a substantial rate of saving, which permitted capital formation based on Japanese rather than foreign investment.

When the Meiji leaders left the scene, the foundations of Japan's industrialization were well laid. Despite cyclical fluctuations, production of goods and services tripled between 1885 and 1935. Railroad building facilitated the growth of a national market. Cotton and steel mills sprang up. Agriculture benefited from chemical fertilizers. The growing population began a steady exodus to the cities, to satisfy the growing demand for factory workers. For five decades, the gross national product (GNP) grew at an average annual rate of 3 percent. The population increased from 33 million to 75 million. Per capita income went up by 2 percent a year. By 1935, industrial products accounted for approximately 70 percent of the GNP.

In short, Japan's economic performance since the early 1950s is not a sudden flash. It is, instead, an accelerated continuation of a process begun a century ago. . . .

A strong foundation alone, however, cannot explain Japan's

pace of development since World War II. Why is it, for instance, that Japan's annual growth rate between 1950 and 1960 was considerably higher than that of the United States, the Soviet Union or the Western European states, with the exception of West Germany? The West German exception suggests part of the answer. As the losers of World War II, both the Germans and the Japanese suffered great destruction of their factories, transportation systems and international trade arrangements. In 1950, the GNP of these states was only a fraction of what it had been in 1940. Economically the Germans and the Japanese began the decade with an abnormally low base line from which to measure their economic growth. In the 1950s Japan was rebuilding what had been destroyed in the war. And again, Japan like West Germany was rich in the most crucial resource—disciplined, skilled, energetic people. In the early 1950s, American economic aid and offshore procurement for the Korean war made vital contributions to Japanese growth. Later in the decade, free-world resources and export markets provided necessary raw materials and outlets for Japanese trade.

In brief, for Japan and West Germany the 1950s were not an economic miracle, but primarily a decade of recovery.

Moreover, recovery is not as simple a notion as one might guess. By 1955 Japan had reached its 1940 GNP, but this did not represent complete recovery. For the 1940 economy, as we have seen, was an expanding, dynamic one. If it had not been for the war destruction, the economy would have continued to grow. Thus, more realistically, recovery can be said to be complete when Japan's GNP reached the level it would have reached if the 1940 economy had kept growing. What this level would be, of course, depends entirely on the projected rate of growth assigned to Japan after 1940. This projected rate of growth rests on so many intangibles that even the most knowledgeable economists can only speculate on what it would have been. In general, however, most economists agree that for Japan, recovery in this sense was not achieved until the early 1960s and that to some extent it might still be going on.

The Phenomenal Sixties

If the 1950–60 growth rate can be understood largely as a result of recovery, American aid, Korean war purchases and the growing availability of foreign resources and markets, what about the phenomenal annual growth rate between 1960 and 1970? How is it that Japan almost quadrupled its GNP in the last ten years, a feat no other developed economy has approached? As we have noted, Japan has continued to be the first in shipbuilding, consolidating itself as the leader in supertanker construction. It has moved rapidly forward to become second in motor vehicle production and computers. This year, Japan's auto makers, led by Toyota and Nissan (manufacturers of Datsuns)—now well-known names in this country—will turn out 5.5 million vehicles, 20 percent of total world production.... During the last ten years Japan also moved past the Western European states, including West Germany, to become third in steel production. Today, American manufacturers import high quality steel from Japan.

To understand this economic record, we should first note that the rate of personal savings and investment in Japan during the past ten years has been higher than in any other industrialized country, accounting for an extraordinary 34 percent of gross capital formation. This means that while wages and consumption have kept pace with productivity, the increasingly affluent Japanese have kept saving and investing at approximately the same rate as they did in the 1920s or the 1950s. In short, the Japanese people, as well as corporations and government, have been plowing their earnings back into growth.

A second major factor has been the effectiveness of government planning and regulation for economic growth. As noted, throughout the past century the government has regulated and encouraged business and industrial development. In the aftermath of World War II, the government's concern with economic growth became a preoccupation. During the 1950s, the Finance Ministry, the Ministry of International Trade and Industry and the Economic Planning Agency recruited the brightest and most promising of the university graduates and put them to work running the economy. While political leaders and bureaucrats in most other states have devoted much of their time and talents to dealing with foreign relations, military affairs and internal political problems, the Japanese have concentrated on economic growth. Throughout the 1960s, it has seemed to Japan's ruling conservatives that this concentration on growth has also been paying domestic political dividends and making sense in foreign affairs.

That the Japanese have been able to devote themselves to economic affairs without being diverted by foreign and military affairs and expenditures is not simply a fortunate accident. It has been a deliberate policy, formulated by Prime Minister Yoshida and his colleagues during the occupation and pursued quietly but consistently by his conservative successors, down to the present prime minister, Eisaku Sato [served 1964–1972]. The United States–Japanese security treaties of 1951 and 1960 have provided an American guarantee against external attack. Shielded by this guarantee, the Japanese government, since the end of the Korean war, has been allocating less than 1 percent of the GNP to military expenditures as opposed to an American outlay averaging 10 percent of GNP. Thus, Japanese economic growth has benefited from the American military presence in Korea, in Japan itself and in the Western Pacific.

A Rosy Outlook

The best-known forecast of Japan's economic future is probably that attributed, somewhat unfairly, to Herman Kahn, director of the Hudson Institute. Mr. Kahn's predictions have actually been greatly qualified. In its widely publicized form, however, the Kahn forecast is a flat assertion that by the end of this [the twentieth] century, Japan will be the greatest economic power in the world, first in GNP and first in per capita income. This forecast is based on a simple projection of Japan's growth rate for the past twenty years. In a nutshell, if the Japanese economy expands at approximately 10 percent per year, and the United States and Soviet economies continue to grow at less than 5 percent per year, before the year 2000 Japan will be outproducing both the present superpowers.

The Economy Stalls

By Marius B. Jansen

Japan's astounding economic rebound in the late 1980s attracted not only widespread admiration but also a great deal of negative response. Trading partners in the West complained that Japan barred imports while exporting goods at prices below what they cost to make. The United States in particular exerted considerable pressure on Japan to open her markets to more than raw materials. All through the 1970s and 1980s, while making some trade concessions, Japan resisted full liberalization. Meanwhile, her trade surpluses and national wealth skyrocketed. At one point, the Tokyo stock market surpassed New York's in value, and land prices reached such a dizzying height that the grounds of the Imperial Palace were said to be worth more than all the real estate in California. Then, with stunning rapidity, everything changed. From the perch of the new century, historian Marius B. Jansen analyzes the rise and fall of Japan's economy and what it means for the future.

For several decades there was a steadily increasing tide of technology introduced—and often improved—in Japan. The U.S. dollar value of items imported, taken by half-decade and beginning in 1949–1955, rose from $69 million to $3.2 billion in the early 1970s, with a tenfold increase in items. In many cases these began as joint ventures with foreign, especially American, firms, and gradually became entirely Japanese as economic power and bureaucratic muscle came to bear.

The result was a surge of exports and a dramatic change in the makeup of those exports. During the 1970s Japan's traditional exports of textiles were matched, and then far exceeded, by the products of heavy industry, of which automobiles were an important part. Television sets and other electronic products grew similarly. Light industries like textiles, Japan's major export for so long, now declined in importance and gradually concentrated on serving the growing home market. Publicists exulted in this growth, and, with thoughts of the urban flowering of Tokugawa times, characterized it as a "new Genroku" [a period from 1688 to 1703 when native arts flourished], or reached back to the dawn of Japanese history to vaunt it as the greatest boom "since [the legendary first emperor] Jimmu." Domestic investment in new and ever larger and more modern plants suggested that Japan was becoming the world's workshop.

Industrial and government leaders, however, continued to warn of Japan's disadvantages in raw materials, in particular its dependence on imported (crude oil) energy, to counter complaints about foreign access to the Japanese market. They feared rising imports as inflationary and evidence of an "overheating" economy, pointing to a basic vulnerability. To some degree their protestations seemed borne out by the early 1980s when the period of high growth came to an end. In 1971 President Nixon moved to end the fixed exchange rates that, at 360 yen to $1, had created so favorable a setting for Japanese exports. The flexible and "floating" exchange rates proved that the yen had indeed been grossly undervalued as it rose to 300, and subsequently peaked at 87 yen to the dollar. Japan was becoming less a protégé of United States policy, and in fact the Nixon administration temporarily prohibited export of soybeans under ancient World War I era legislation banning trade with "enemy nations."

Oil Shock

Worse was to come as Near Eastern instability brought about the first oil crisis, which increased (in dollars) the price of oil fourfold. The oil crisis created a sense of national emergency. Government and industry leaders orchestrated a skillful campaign for the conservation of energy. The lights of the metropolis were suddenly dimmed. Police checked implementation of restrictions on heating and air conditioning in office buildings. Radio, television, and the press reminded housewives of the importance of saving energy. Planning and moralizing combined to limit the damage of the oil shock, and by the time a second round of shortages struck at the height of the Iranian revolution in 1978, Japan, though no less dependent on oil imports than it had been before, was better prepared to deal with it than many of its industrial competitors. Meanwhile the export of fuel-efficient vehicles flourished.

As Japan's export surpluses grew, pressure came from many countries, but especially from the United States, for trade liberalization and better access to the Japanese market. Japanese government negotiators moved slowly and grudgingly, raising the possibility of a domestic backlash as a deterrent, while their Washington counterparts warned of the possibility of protectionist legislation in the United States Congress in response to job loss. In fact, however, the security tie with Japan was so vital to Washington strategists that successive administrations were able to head off advocates of protectionism. Frequently the Japanese government, even more anxious to head off such legislation, committed itself to voluntary export restrictions (VERs) under which industrial export quotas were allocated to exporters. One might consider this an updated version of the "gentleman's agreement" earlier in the century by which the Japanese government had sought to ease frictions caused by immigration earlier in the century. It was an interim and unsatisfactory system, however, for it had the effect of strengthening the governmental role despite regular American requests for reducing it.

As Japanese exports increased, there was widespread admiration for their management systems that seemed to result in products of high quality with a minimum of labor disputes. "Permanent employment" that secured jobs and eased fears of technological innovation, a seniority system of pay that guaranteed equity, and "quality control circles" that institutionalized worker participation in shop-floor decisions seemed the harbingers of a more humane and rewarding system. Management, not subject to quarterly bottom-line judgments on profits, was able to plan for a longer future, and that future seemed one of indefinite expansion and growth. It was particularly the employment and management systems that attracted attention.

Quality Guru for Japan

Japanese and American publicists credited a good deal of this to the role of an American management consultant, W. Edwards Deming, who visited Japan at the end of the Occupation and returned periodically thereafter. Deming, credited with formative influence on the postwar Japanese economy through his emphasis on quality control, was depicted as the prophet of the new industrial order, and journalists in the United States lamented that it was Japanese management, rather than American, that had heeded his advice. Japanese journalists also lauded him as a great teacher from abroad. It is probable that Deming's emergence as imported icon needs to be placed in a context that includes Ernest Fenollosa and other Meiji instructors, Chinese painters at Nagasaki who were hailed as great teachers, and Buddhist evangelists like Ganjin much earlier. More sober evaluations serve to condition these assessments. Lifetime employment and seniority pay were recent and not traditional Japanese patterns. They were furthermore restricted to approximately one-quarter of the labor force. Nor did Deming's management philosophy spring full-blown from the ashes of World War II, for Japanese managers had followed Western and particularly American management philosophy, including "Taylorism," since prewar days. As with Fenollosa, it was rather the fortuitous appearance of a foreign voice that could be credited with inspiring trends that benefited Japan and pleased the outside world; this resulted in the elevation of Deming to near-mythological status.

The economies of South Korea, Taiwan, Hong Kong, and Singapore seemed to be taking Japan as their model, and in the 1980s interest in a "Japanese miracle" was followed by talk of an "Asian miracle." Japanese banks and enterprises made massive investments in Southeast Asia and—less so—in China, and some grumbled that the Co-Prosperity Sphere was being realized after all. Speculative expansion fueled the Tokyo stock market to an unprecedented height. Banks, awash with capital, competed for borrowers uncritically and poured their resources into other lending institutions that were even less discriminating. Real estate prices became astronomical and minute plots were said to bring prices wildly out of range at any comparative level. Japanese firms purchased signature properties in the United States and Europe, and individual buyers drove the market for Impressionist paintings at auctions throughout the West. Japan, so long a debtor nation, became the largest creditor nation in the world; Japanese purchases of United States Treasury notes subsidized the budget deficits of the 1980s, and now it was the United States that was the world's largest debtor nation. It seemed to some that the Japanese had developed a new variety of capitalism. Deferred gratification, long-range planning with bureaucratic encouragement, and harmonious relations between labor and management in the furtherance of the "house" or enterprise had brought Japan prosperity with remarkably equitable income distribution.

All this stood in contrast to the ruthlessly competitive forces un-leashed by an American-style free market.

The Bubble Bursts

And then, in the last decade of the century, the "bubble," that classic symbol of arrogance, conceit, and overconfidence in seventeenth-century Dutch genre paintings, burst. In the early months of the last decade of the century the Tokyo stock market index fell from 33,000 to 13,000. Economic growth declined sharply, then became flat and even negative, and Japan entered a decade of deep recession, the most serious since the war. The economic institutions and tactics that had seemed so strong proved remarkably resistant to altered circumstances; it turned out that it was easier to encourage growth from a modest level than it was to sustain growth in a mature economy. Early steps in lib-eralization sometimes led to massive errors in judgment; stories of materialism, greed, and corruption greeted newspaper readers day after day. Observers who had sought the elements involved in Japanese success now wondered why the new situation was rec-ognized so late, and why corrective steps were so slow in coming.

One can say that the bubble burst of its own momentum and that valuations of real estate and equities had reached prices that were wildly out of touch with profits and reality. As the specu-lative fever rose, bad money had followed good; organized crime vaulted beyond its usual sphere of protection rackets to join the real estate and securities frenzy, and careless lending practices led to multiple liens on many commercial properties which now be-came targets for squatters and furtive, fictive corporations.

Rash misjudgment in economic decisions brought with it equally rash and brazen corruption in politics. A series of highly publicized scandals revealed ties between LDP leaders, construc-tion interests, and campaign funding that helped unseat the LDP and led to the establishment of the Hosokawa cabinet.

Next came the Asian economic crisis. In many countries of Southeast Asia the flood of foreign investment capital had come before regulatory rules of transparency had been established, cre-ating personal and familial political empires that proved fragile.

These events struck giant Japanese banks that had become some of the world's largest financial institutions. The collapse of the real estate market left a plethora of nonperforming loans, and the Asian crisis intensified the banks' misfortunes. Soon they were scrambling to meet regulatory requirements for liquid assets, and efforts to include in such reports the (now depreciated) equities of client firms whose equities they held raised fears about the larger financial system. The government allowed several banks, among them the Long-Term Credit Bank, to fall, and tightened its requirements for reports. Toward the end of the decade a massive infusion of public money began to stabilize the banks. Analysts noted that the crisis was more extended, more expensive, and its solution less thoroughgoing than the process whereby the United States government had dealt with American savings and loans institutions a few years earlier.

A Faltering Economy

During all this businessmen found themselves unable to borrow money and the economy slowly ground to a halt. Government measures reduced the interest rate to the world's lowest—0.25 percent—but that made it the more necessary to borrow and less rewarding to save and lend. Outsiders had seen Japanese recovery as leading that of Asia, but Japan, so recently the locomotive of Asian growth, seemed instead the caboose. Now the institutions on which so much had been predicated, particularly permanent employment and seniority pay, stood in the way of the restructuring and rationalization that the United States economy experienced in the 1980s. These brief paragraphs can only begin to suggest the complexity of the interrelationships at work, but they may suffice to explain the toll the decade of the 1990s took on the shibboleths of the 1980s: wise bureaucrats, cautious leaders, far-sighted planners, and familial consensus.

At century's end the Japanese government responded with impressive efforts to stimulate economic activity through public spending on infrastructure. Few streams remained unbridged, few shores lacked bulwarks, and the countryside changed as contractors searched for highways to repave. The return of free-spending habits nevertheless remained out of reach; instead consumers saved for an uncertain future. Japan's savings rate, always high, passed 20 percent, while America's, where confidence grew, entered the negative column.

A final and perhaps serious factor was that Japanese costs had outrun productivity gains. The years of the 1970s and 1980s left the country with price and salary levels that made Japan less competitive than it had been. Major Japanese exporters were moving production facilities to other shores. Within Japan a web of institutions and regulations that favored agriculture and small shops combined with a distribution system to keep prices the world's highest. Salaries were high, but prices even higher. This, at a time when the flow of the postwar generation into retirement was about to put maximum pressure on savings and pension provisions, promised more problems for the new century.

Foreign Takeovers

Remarkably, however, economic distress also brought with it relaxation of long-standing curbs on foreign investment. When a major Japanese brokerage house entered bankruptcy it was taken over by a New York firm. When the giant automobile maker Nissan found itself unable to borrow money in Japan it turned to the French government and Renault for a solution. The Ford Motor Company gained control of Mazda, Daimler-Chrysler negotiated with Mitsubishi Motors. New York financial institutions sent squadrons of executives to buy up real estate at bargain rates.

A thoroughgoing solution, if one was to be found, thus required more transparency, greater freedom from administrative guidance, and a more sensitive response to international trends and examples. Such globalization, however, would bring in train further rationalization, reduction of productive capacity, and a threat to the web—or womb—of security and safety that the postwar Japanese economy had made for itself. The social and political consequences of this were unclear; the Japanese establishment was not prepared to surrender unconditionally to the "rational choice" posed so confidently by overseas consultants....

The long sway of the Liberal Democratic Party ended when a Diet vote of no confidence toppled the Miyazawa government in 1993, and for a brief moment a "reform" administration under Hosokawa Morihiro, wildly popular in Japan and welcomed overseas, held out the hope of a new politics. Before the Hosokawa cabinet fell, as it soon did, an electoral system in place since the 1920s had been reshaped and the import of rice, long banned, became possible.

Then came the full consequences of the bubble economy that had burst; revelation of scandals, dishonesty, clumsy delay in taking remedial steps, bankruptcies, threats to job security, and rising unemployment all combined to shake faith in the wisdom and integrity of Japan's long-respected bureaucrats. Japanese investors beat a hasty retreat from the signature properties in the United States whose purchase had alarmed Americans. Additional problems related to Japan's success in treating public health and improving the environment. The Japanese population was living longer and also aging rapidly, and the system of health insurance and social security support was coming under heavy strain. A generation of Japanese was moving toward retirement, and their pension funds, given the puny interest rate that would prevail for a decade, offered little guaranty for the future. Economic recovery became ever more urgent, at home and abroad.

Japanese Resilience

Clearly there was no lack of problems facing Japan as it entered the new millennium. . . . Japan is fated to become once again an active participant in world affairs. Its Security Treaty with the United States holds good, but in the absence of the former Soviet threat its priority must decline. Yet this is not to suggest a new military role, for Japan's abhorrence of war seems deep and firm. Nevertheless American hegemony will lessen, and some new balance of the United States, Russia, China, Japan, and one or both Koreas must emerge.

Japan's society has shown enormous resilience and strength in the past millennium. A thousand years ago the court society of Lady Murasaki's *Tale of Genji* was giving way to that of warriors whose rule was fastened on the country for eight hundred years. The Meiji revolution disarmed those samurai and armed the state instead. The new Meiji empire flourished briefly, but in defeat that state was itself disarmed. Reconstruction brought enormous economic influence and power, but that structure too was not immune to cyclical decline. Yet no student of the Japanese past could doubt that a nation so gifted, resourceful, and courageous was destined to play a major role in the millennium now begun.

THE HISTORY OF NATIONS
Chapter 6

Japan's Clouded Future

Three Driving Forces

BY DAVID J. STALEY

Historians recognize that no single factor can account for all changes in a complex society. At any given moment, various forces tug in various directions. Japan's penchant for making sudden changes while hanging on to its cultural traditions makes forecasting its future especially difficult. Still, some winds of change blow harder than others. In Japan, the pressing need to further reform the economy, the rapid aging of the population, and the rise of a new and rather different generation of postwar Japanese all point the way to inevitable changes. In this article, historian David J. Staley attempts to gauge the impact of these three major trends on Japan's future.

Japan is crossing a threshold from one historic period into another but is uncertain which potential new era will emerge. The outcome will affect everyone in an increasingly globalized future.

After rising from the rubble of World War II, Japan prospered from 1960 to the late 1990s. Now that period of prosperity appears to have come to an end. Those three decades were characterized by Japan's economic resurgence, high growth rates, a dedicated and group-oriented workforce, economic nationalism, relative cultural homogeneity, and a social structure that retained many of its premodern features, especially with regard to gender roles and family structure.

The task of this article is to imagine the other side of this threshold, to inquire as to what the "next period" in Japanese social history may look like.

The convergence of three large-scale driving forces will determine the resulting shape of Japanese society in this next period. These driving forces are the restructuring of the Japanese

David J. Staley, "Japan's Uncertain Future: Key Trends and Scenarios," *The Futurist*, vol. 36, March/April 2002, pp. 48–52. Copyright © 2002 by World Future Society. Reproduced by permission.

economy, the long-term effects of demographic change, and the coming of age of the generation known as the "new breed."

• Restructuring of the Japanese economy. The economic downturn of the 1990s seems to be having more profound effects than simply a downturn in the value of the yen or of the real estate market. The systems of lifetime employment, of devoted "salarymen" who overworked themselves for the good of corporation and country, and of capitalism dominated by corporate bureaucrats and government ministers have been seriously undermined. Japan is losing its hold as a leading economy and is instead chasing the rest of the industrialized world.

• The long-term effects of demographic change. By the first quarter of the twenty-first century, a significant portion of Japan's population will be over 65 years old and the birthrate will hover very close to 0%. These demographic trends will influence both the economy and the social, cultural, and familial institutions of Japan. Older Japanese will need to be cared for; no system of social security of the American or European variety now exists. The burden may well fall to families, specifically to women. The slower birthrates and grayer population will put pressure on labor markets, as companies scramble to find enough skilled and unskilled workers.

• The coming of age of the generation the Japanese refer to as the "new breed." These are the children of the postwar generation that rebuilt Japan with their hard work and self-sacrifice. This younger generation has not known poverty, or even deep economic recession. Critics complain that they are not as devoted and driven as their parents, and are content to enjoy the benefits of materialism and consumerism. They appear more individualistic than earlier generations, less willing to sacrifice for the group. Older Japanese find them rude and without values.

At the same time, the new breed appear more cosmopolitan, more accepting of outsiders, and less bound by traditional gender assumptions. This generation may well hold the key to the shape of the next period in Japanese history. As they mature and assume positions of responsibility, the new breed may govern Japan in a radically different fashion than previous generations. On the other hand, like American baby boomers who were radical in their youth but who acted more like their parents as they matured, the Japanese new breed could begin to think and act as their parents and grandparents did, making the next period in

Japanese history far from a radical break.

The effects of these three driving forces—economic restructuring, aging population, and "new breed" generation—will not be felt in isolation. Rather, the confluence and collision of these forces will spin off the effects that will characterize this next period. What follows are four plausible "next periods" covering the coming 20–25 years of Japan's future.

Entrepreneurial Japan

Group identification and self-sacrifice were important keys to the postwar reconstruction of Japan, but with the downturn of the 1990s, the Japanese government has perceived the need for more individual initiative in order to bolster Japan's economy and to make it competitive once again. The government has begun to sponsor schools that will teach entrepreneurship. Talented individuals aspiring to be infotech entrepreneurs are flocking to American universities, bypassing Tokyo University, the traditional training ground of the Japanese elite. In effect, Japan is borrowing the idea of entrepreneurship from the West, specifically from the United States.

An entrepreneurial Japan might take one of two forms. In one scenario, entrepreneurship remains wedded to the corporate structure, assuming the form of "intrapreneurship." Rather than allowing talented individuals to form their own companies, established companies harness the creativity and risk-taking initiatives of young entrepreneurs to their own corporate decision-making structures. The corporation rewards not the team but individuals, through promotions. However, the economic benefits of risk taking continue to go to the company, not to the individual.

In an alternative version of this scenario, Japan borrows an entrepreneurial culture that looks more American than Japanese. Japanese schools emphasize creativity and problem solving rather than rote memorization, in order to more fully develop the individual rather than a team worker. Individualistic young adults from the "new breed" generation break away from the large corporations, build their own firms, and reap the benefits for themselves. In this scenario, the energy and dynamism of the Japanese economy comes from risk takers rather than from the long-term planning of corporate and ministerial bureaucrats.

Today, conspicuous consumption and social differentiation based on wealth or income are looked down upon in Japan. But a new entrepreneurial Japan might produce a "cult of the entrepreneur," where the individual visionary is lionized in the popular mind, rewarded for his initiative, and envied for his wealth. We may well see in the next 25 years a growing number of Japanese Bill Gateses.

Quality of Life

Borrowing entrepreneurship might allow Japan to regain its pre-1990 level of global economic dominance. Although the Japanese economy is no longer "number one," it is easy to imagine that it might again rise to this level. Another plausible scenario, however, sees Japan as a second-tier economy, wealthy and healthy, but not a global economic leader. Like the Scandinavian countries or Great Britain, this Japan retains high rates of literacy, comfortable standards of living, and long average life-spans; Japanese workers begin to value the quality of life more than before.

The current wave of layoffs has been a shock to post–World War II Japan, as many companies appear to be abandoning the central tenet of the Japanese social contract: lifetime employment. That might explain the apparent apathy of the new-breed generation. Unlike their parents, Japanese young adults today do not expect lifelong employment and are wary about loyalties to companies and institutions that might easily abandon them.

In this scenario, the decline in company loyalty leads to a decline in productivity. Workers no longer possess a single-minded devotion to the success of the company, a major factor in Japan's postwar boom and position of economic leadership. Thus Japan's economy fails to regain its position as number one even while providing a comfortable lifestyle for its citizens.

As the movement toward a concern for quality of life grows, Japanese workers develop a greater concern for lifestyle issues than for company success. The result is an increase in recreation, shopping, and other pursuits, including more profound uses of leisure time. In this scenario, Japan witnesses a spiritual revival, and more and more Japanese pursue traditional pastimes, such as flower arranging and Noh theater.

A noteworthy feature of this scenario is the awakening of Japanese fathers. The time that workers might have spent on the job or socializing and team building with cohorts is instead given over to the enjoyment of family. Led by the new breed, men take on greater responsibilities for raising their children.

An Inclusive Society

Japanese women today have more theoretical rights granted in their constitution than women in the United States. However, in practice, Japanese women have little role in public affairs, the halls of government, or the boardrooms of corporations. Women in the workplace typically occupy lower-level clerical positions, usually in service to men. They are expected to leave the company once they are married and if they are pregnant. Inside companies and in popular images in the mass media, women are perceived as cute and decorative. The widespread use of "hostesses" by male executives and the ubiquity of miniskirt-clad pixies in Japanese cartoons symbolize the subservient status of women in contemporary Japan.

As its population grays and as its birthrates continue to fall, Japan faces a potential shortage of both skilled and unskilled labor. In the Inclusive Society scenario, women are called upon to help make up the deficit. In order to make this possible, women are freed from the sole responsibility for childrearing; their husbands share more familial responsibilities. Many couples bring their children to work, as child-care facilities become standard in all workplaces. Since women no longer have to leave work after they marry or have children, they remain in the workplace longer and ascend to positions of responsibility and leadership. Government and business leaders begin to recognize the value of this heretofore untapped pool of human capital.

Like American and European women who assumed male responsibilities in wartime, Japanese women's participation in the workforce is vital to the nation. They begin to insist upon rewards for their services, including real equality rather than the paper equality promised in the Japanese constitution. Public groping of women—formerly accepted as a kind of "boys will be boys" prank—is no longer tolerated by either men or women. Like the samurai, hostesses become a relic of the Japanese past, popular in novels and movies but no longer a real presence.

Women begin to assume leadership positions among the powerful ministerial bureaucracies and multinational corporations, the seats of real power in Japan. A woman is elected prime minister, and women begin to lead the influential Bank of Japan and the Ministry of International Trade and Industry.

Another way the Japanese might head off a projected labor shortage would be through the use of immigrant labor. The rise in the number of immigrant workers, coupled with the younger generation's more cosmopolitan outlook, might produce a more multicultural society in Japan.

Japan has long had a love/hate relationship with foreigners. While the Japanese have craved foreign goods, labor, and expertise, they have treated foreigners as outsiders. But in this scenario, as more immigrants arrive in Japan to fill job vacancies, they are gradually welcomed more formally into Japanese society. Immigrants are invited not only for their labor but to settle and establish families. Native Japanese warm to the presence of foreigners in their midst and welcome their food, customs, and culture, blending them with their own. Foods that once were unfamiliar become staples of the Japanese diet; like pizza in the United States, foods that were once foreign become redefined as "Japanese." The definition of Japanese is widened to include other people from Asia as well as Westerners.

As they gain positions of influence, the more cosmopolitan new-breed generation adopts new policies that encourage more foreigners to reside in Japan. The traditional restrictions against citizenship are increasingly relaxed. Personal relationships and marriages between Japanese and non-Japanese become more commonplace.

Return to Isolation?

The same demographic forces that allow for greater gender equality and multiculturalism may also harden traditional attitudes toward women and outsiders. It is tempting to assume that, because Japan is a modern industrial economy, its society and culture will inevitably begin to look more Western. However, it is just as plausible that demographic pressures might induce a conservative social reaction.

In the retrenchment scenario, Japanese corporations continue their long-established practice of using industrial robots to fill the gap in both skilled and unskilled labor, rather than filling vacancies with women. This machine labor is supplemented by an increase in immigrant labor.

Where women's labor will see growing demand in this scenario is in the care of the nation's elderly. Because the population is graying, more and more Japanese seniors need to be cared for. In the absence of assisted-living centers or a reliable system of social security, the burden for the care of the elderly falls upon families—its traditional source—and especially upon women.

More pressing is the need for children. Japanese birthrates, as with all other advanced industrial societies, have been falling throughout the past 100 years. In this scenario, the government seeks both formal and informal means to raise the Japanese birthrate. Amid fears of the "death of Japanese culture," official policies encourage couples to have many children. Women are encouraged to remain at home to raise children. Women who decide to remain childless or unmarried face shame and ridicule. Work outside the home is out of the question except in a few cases, and largely for young single women who will be expected to leave the workplace once they are married. Public opinion discourages women from seeking higher-status jobs in favor of the patriotic duties of motherhood. While many of the social abuses of women are eliminated, such as groping and unflattering mass media images, women remain second-class citizens whose public activities are circumscribed.

The increase in the number of foreigners in Japan might have the effect of hardening traditional restrictions on and wariness of outsiders. In this scenario, Japan is not isolated from international trade, though it does adopt policies aimed at cultural isolation, including linguistically.

The presence of larger numbers of outsiders—made necessary because of demographic pressures and labor shortages—has a disquieting effect on the society at large. Conservatives who fear the death of Japanese culture increasingly speak of "a thinning of Japanese blood." The foreigners who do come to Japan are isolated and ghettoized by the society at large.

The boundary separating the Japanese from other groups remains firm. Discrimination against Koreans and Chinese continues, taking on newer, subtler forms. While there are no official policies, adults place informal pressures on young people to keep them from interacting with foreigners, and intermarriage is looked down upon. Citizenship requirements are very strict. Those foreigners who do intermarry produce children who are discriminated against.

Externally, Japan fights to maintain its status as an island nation. Like the protectionism in the 1980s, which sought to shield Japanese industries from free trade, Japan seeks similar policies to protect its native culture. Although telecommunications makes the world seem more global, in this scenario information from the outside remains much more restricted than in Western nations. By not learning new languages, most Japanese are cut off from a significant portion of international communications. While setting up protectionist cultural policies, the Japanese attempt to export their culture to the rest of the world, especially their popular culture. Regional neighbors are looked at with suspicion; while only a handful of militants speak of a revival of empire, most Japanese affect a detached attitude toward regional alliances. Japan opts out of the global village.

A Generational Choice

The final shape of the next period of Japanese social history will be determined by how the three large-scale driving forces of economic restructuring, demographic change, and the new-breed generation converge. Of the three, the new-breed generation holds an important key. As they enter positions of authority and responsibility, the actions, behaviors, and choices of this generation will determine if Japan's future is more Western, inclusive, and global or neonationalist and culturally isolated. Despite its recent economic setbacks, Japan remains an important player in the global economic system. The next period of Japanese history will therefore have ramifications for all of us affected by that system.

Pluralistic Japan: Coming to Terms with Racial and Ethnic Diversity

By Gavan McCormack

Japan's national mythology of one family tracing its origin back to the Sun Goddess has led the government, scholars, and gullible outsiders to deny the very existence of ethnic minorities in Japan. Yet culturally and even racially distinct minorities, such as the Ainu people of Northern Japan and the Ryukyu people of the southern isle of Okinawa, are part of Japan's past and present. So, too, are Korean immigrants, as well as more recent arrivals from all over Asia and the larger world beyond. Japan's growing recognition of the need to become more internationally minded has created pressures at home to acknowledge domestic diversity. In the following excerpts from an introduction to a book on multiculturalism in Japan, historian Gavan McCormack highlights the recent observations of scholars re-examining the nation's historical and future diversity.

Japan is conventionally seen as a monocultural society. Located at the eastern extremity of the Eurasian land-mass and separated from it by a sea that is wider and more dangerous than that which divides the British Isles from the same land-mass at its western extremity, it is apparently distinguished from the countries nearest to it both in its pre-modern institutions (often called 'feudal') and in its modern economic dynamism (sometimes called 'miraculous'). The proposition that Japan is unique and monocultural seems plausible.

Throughout Japanese history, prominent figures have insisted on the distinctness of Japanese identity, from the 'National Learning' (*Kokugakusha*) scholars in the eighteenth century with their stress on a pure and untrammeled (that is, non-Chinese) Japanese essence to late twentieth-century statements by Nakasone Yasuhiro (Prime Minister in the 1980s) that Japan is a homogeneous 'natural community' (as distinct from a Western-style 'nation formed by contract'), and the 'Yamato race' which he insisted had been living 'for at least two thousand years . . . hand in hand with no other, different ethnic groups present [in these islands]'. The belief that Japan is a homogeneous, monoracial state is deep-rooted and, as Ivan Hall notes, has long been 'openly sanctioned by the intellectual establishment, public consensus, and government policy'. Unlike other societies which are mixed *(o-majiri)*, especially the United States with its [as Nakasone put it] 'many Blacks, Puerto Ricans and Mexicans', Japan is thought to be pure and homogeneous, and therefore to have had an easier time becoming an 'intelligent society'.

A National Family

In the modern (pre-1945) state, the ideology of Japanese homogeneity and superiority was encapsulated in what was described as *kokutai* (national polity), by which the Japanese people were seen as a unique family state united around the emperor. Though discredited by defeat and the collapse of imperial Japan and the Greater East Asia Co-Prosperity Sphere (but not of the imperial line nor of its myths), neither the Occupation nor the postwar Japanese liberal and progressive forces paid much attention to questions of identity. The former concentrated on eradicating militarism while shoring up the imperial institution, and the latter on analysing class while ignoring ethnicity and assuming that a strengthening of individualism and democracy would result from steadily increasing modernisation. The ethnic implications of the aboriginal inhabitants of Japan (the Ainu), or other groups such as the large Korean minority, were reduced to considerations of universal human rights. Deep-rooted assumptions about 'Japaneseness' therefore survived intact.

From the 1980s two phenomena have proceeded on parallel tracks which show no sign of converging: internationalisation and the clarification of Japanese identity. *Kokusaika*—internationalisation—has been a Japanese national goal for over a decade. Trans-border flows of capital, goods, technology and people have reached new heights, and essays and books on *koku-saika* proliferate. For all of this inter-meshing with the outside world, the task of analysing 'Japaneseness', and how notions of it might be reconciled with a *kokusaika* world, remains both complex and sensitive. The stronger the belief in Japanese distinctiveness, the deeper became the concern at the consequences of 'internationalisation' as economic super-power status led to the opening, first of the economy and then of the society, and an influx of migrant workers.

Back to Jōmon

This desire to clarify identity is the local manifestation of the worldwide phenomenon of identity politics. During the 1980s Japan's roots were increasingly traced back to the Jōmon hunting and gathering culture which lasted for about 10 000 years prior to the fourth century BC. Influential statements of the 'true' untrammeled Japanese identity in such terms have been uttered by prominent academics and by political figures such as Ozawa Ichirō, who revealed his romantic inclinations by declaring that Jōmon Japan was not only Japan's own true essence but also the solution to the problems of contemporary civilisation. . . .

It now seems clear that the Japanese population stems from several ancient and distinct waves of immigration. An early (but not necessarily the first) was that of a proto-Mongoloid people from somewhere in the South-east Asian or South China region who (by a route yet unclear) settled in the islands at some point in the Palaeolithic. The civilisation of hunters and gatherers that evolved has been given the name 'Jōmon' after the cord-marked pattern of their earthenware pottery.

Unlike the first wave of immigrants, whose physical characteristics suggest close links with South-east Asia or South China, the second came from North-east Asia, most likely via the Korean peninsula. This migration continued for over a millennium through what are known as the Yayoi and Kofun periods (*ca.* 400 BC to AD 700), and by the latter (Kofun) period there seems to have been considerable mixing of indigenous and immigrant groups as far as southern Tohoku. About a million people left the continent in some 'boat people' saga whose causes are only dimly understood, to settle in the archipelago, until eventually the original Jōmon peoples were outnumbered, perhaps by as much as 10 to 1 (according to Hanihara Kazurō). The archipelago was profoundly transformed as a result. The migrants brought wet rice agriculture and bronze and iron technology. They settled first in northern Kyushu and western Honshu, either merging with and absorbing the aboriginal Jōmon inhabitants or confining them to culturally distinctive formations in the 'peripheral' regions of Hokkaido and Northern Honshu (where they appeared thereafter as Ainu, Emishi, Ebisu) or South Kyushu and the Ryūkyū Islands (where they were known as Kumaso, Hayato, as well as Okinawan). By the seventh century, these North-east Asian immigrants and their descendants constituted between 70 and 90 per cent of the population of the islands (which might by then have amounted to five or six million people), and constructed a distinctive political and cultural order centering on the court which emerged in the Kinai region in the vicinity of present-day Osaka and Kyoto.

Racial Purity Debunked

As Katayama notes, relatively pure Jōmon characteristics were preserved only in the Ainu communities in the far north. Skeletal, dental and genetic anthropology, and the analysis of the genetic evidence of the different origins of animals closely connected with human habitation, such as dogs and mice, make clear that the modern Japanese are primarily descended from continental immigrants who arrived in the Yayoi and Kofun periods. The idea of a uniquely pure link between the modern Japanese and the ancient civilisation of the Jōmon period cannot be sustained. The Japanese are, like all other modern peoples, a 'mixed race'....

When Okinawa and Hokkaido were absorbed within the Japanese state in the late nineteenth century their inhabitants, despite being redefined as 'Japanese citizens', nevertheless remained *different* in ways which disturbed official constructions of national uniformity. Ultimately they were redefined as different in terms of time rather than space: as 'backward' rather than foreign. But this process was not without risk, for it might imply that they represented a 'purer' or more 'pristine' expression of 'essential' 'Japaneseness'. Japanese debates about terms such as 'race' *(jinshu)* and *'Volk' (minzoku)* therefore focus on these peoples....

The Rest of Asia

If Hokkaido and Okinawa constitute internal benchmarks of Japanese identity, Korea, China and South-east Asia all represent facets of the Japanese struggle to achieve an outward-looking, non-Western sense of identity that would combine 'Japanese-ness', 'Asian-ness', and universal human values. . . .

Japan launched its Asian war beneath slogans of 'co-existence and co-prosperity, respect for autonomy and independence, and the abolition of racial discrimination', but under the veneer of these universal values lay a Japanese belief in the 'low cultural level' of the natives, and in practice, relations between Japan and the worlds it was supposedly liberating fell far short of the ideals. Official constructions of modern Japanese identity were always fraught with tensions, which became increasingly evident in the years leading up to the Pacific War. Government policy since the Meiji Restoration had been founded upon emulation of the western great powers. Its aim was the transformation of Japan into an industrialised, militarily powerful nation with its own colonial empire to rival those of Britain and France. As conflict with the west grew, however, Japan's leaders revised the earlier strategy of 'leaving Asia and joining Europe' *(datsu-A nyū-O)*, proposing instead to rejoin Asia on whose behalf it would lead a crusade against 'western imperialism'.

The unresolved contradictions of coloniser-liberator became ever more apparent as the war progressed. [A Japanese historian] vividly illustrates the ironies of Japan's position by examining the role of Indonesia in the Greater East Asian Co-Prosperity Sphere. Entangled by long-held views of Southeast Asia as a 'bar-barian' realm, pragmatic desires to exploit the resources of the re-gion, and a Pan-Asian rhetoric which defined Japan as the 'lib-erator' of Asia, the Japanese military were unable either to treat Indonesia as an equal or entirely to suppress nationalist demands for independence.

Japan's colonial role raised fundamental questions about the definition of the word 'Japanese'. Japan's self-proclaimed mission as 'liberator of Asia' sat uncomfortably with its role as colonial ruler in Korea. The Japanese government tried to blur this con-tradiction by defining its status in Korea, not as imperialist, but as 'elder brother' nurturing the development of 'younger brother'. This imagery was supported by assimilationist policies imposed on the Koreans, who were enlisted in the Japanese armed forces and enrolled in the family registration system (*koseki*), albeit in a special category which marked them as 'overseas residents'. But the people who were 'Japanese' when it came to military service suddenly ceased to be 'Japanese' after the post-war peace settlement, and were thus deprived of their entitlement to Japanese war and disability pensions. In a final irony, as Utsumi points out, Korean recruits to the Japanese military were deemed by the Allies to be liable for prosecution for war crimes, on the basis of 'Japanese nationality' of which they had since been stripped. So the paradoxes of war created human tragedies whose consequences continue to colour Japan's relations with the Asian region to the present day. . . .

A New Diversity

This [viewpoint] can only hint at the richness of Japan's multiculturalist tradition. However, the creation of a multicultural future depends on, and is fed by, the discovery of the multiculturalism of the past. While the monolithic and homogeneous myths of the past served the interests of elites intent on preserving order and control, helping to legitimise established authority, the common people preserved rich and diverse counter-traditions, which were open, bridged social and class distinctions, and had little time for the pretensions of their rulers. From the mountain and seafaring peoples discussed by Amino, through the mediaeval and early modern-urban, mass religious movements, to the contemporary peoples living on the Japanese periphery—such as the 'Yaponesia' (or 'Okinesia') vision described by Hanazaki—they understood the priority of universal, human, moral qualities over the particularistic, ethnic or racial qualities of 'Japaneseness'.

An ideology rooted in the myths of uniqueness and the 'pure' blood tradition is still proclaimed, often stridently, by representatives of the tradition of centralised authority, but the foundations on which they stand are crumbling. From the 1980s a new wave of foreigners, attracted by Japan's prosperity, began to pour into Japan's cities, while the villages (where 'pure' 'Japaneseness' was supposed to be concentrated), suffering depopulation as a result of urban-oriented growth and desperate to find brides for young farmers, began to import brides from China, Korea, the Philippines, Thailand and Sri Lanka. The number of Japanese citizens living abroad, many of them married to foreigners, also increased dramatically. A new stage of hybridisation of culture was underway, carrying with it positive potential for opening, globalising, and achieving *kokusaika* (even if not of the kind desired by cultural mandarins). To carry the process through will require sloughing off the cocoon of Japanese uniqueness. In the 1300-year history of the 'Japanese' state, centralised political authority has been the exception rather than the rule, surviving less than a hundred years of the *ritsuryō* state of the seventh to eighth century and the 'modern' state from 1868. For most of its history, Japan has been a highly decentralised state and society. The consciousness that there was any coherent 'Japan' (a 'Nihonkoku') at all was born, not of the *diktat* of central authorities, but rather of the pilgrimages of monks, the journeying of merchants, and the wanderings of travelling artists. The diverse traditions of the archipelago may flourish again as the current phase of centralised authority is also transcended.

Searching for a New Global Role

By GILBERT ROZMAN

For most of the postwar era, Japan concentrated on building its economic power. It gained a worldwide reputation for manufacturing and exporting high-quality industrial and consumer goods. In foreign policy, however, it was largely content to remain under the protective wing of the United States. At home, most of the population, recalling the catastrophe of World War II, regarded nationalism and especially militarism with deep suspicion. Abroad, Japan had little desire to be on the front lines of conflict, whether in the Middle East, where it looked for vital oil imports, or the Asian mainland, where neighbors still nursed grudges from ill treatment at the hands of Japan's Imperial Army and Navy. In the 1980s, however, Japan's foreign policy outlook began to change. Japanese leaders believed their nation's prosperity could translate into peaceful political power on the world stage. In the following excerpts from a 2002 article in the foreign policy journal Orbis, *Gilbert Rozman, senior fellow at the Philadelphia-based Foreign Policy Research Center, evaluates Japan's efforts to increase its role in international affairs.*

Japanese foreign policy in the middle of 2001 was in utter disarray. The Japanese media resorted to terms such as pandemonium, paralysis, terror, and war. Makiko Tanaka's idiosyncrasy as foreign minister in the new [cabinet of Prime Minister] Junichiro Koizumi ... accounted for some but not all of the turmoil. Detractors charged her with creating havoc on the basis of a "daughter's vengeance" and a "housewife's feelings" and undertaking a coup d'état against the bureaucratic system. In fact she had found herself in the midst of an enormous muddle. As professionals called for urgent action to restore a consensus and stem the damage to the national interest, advocates pleaded for a new direction to overcome the lethargy of a decade of inertia

Gilbert Rozman, "Japan's Quest for Great Power Identity," *Orbis*, vol. 46, Winter 2002, pp. 73–91. Copyright © 2002 by the Foreign Policy Research Institute. Reproduced by permission.

that could cause still more harm. To determine how Japan might extricate itself from this situation we must first understand what precipitated it.

In their March [2001] meetings in Irkutsk, Prime Minister Yoshiro Mori and Russian president Vladimir Putin had moved boldly toward a breakthrough in relations. The result was a national outcry to the effect that Mori was reversing Japan's long-standing negotiating position without building domestic support or understanding how this departure might actually cause a new crisis in Japanese-Russian relations. Mori's decision the next month to permit a visit by former Taiwan president Lee Teng-hui for medical reasons met with general approval, although many warned of the impact on relations with China, which had already been rocked by Japan's imposition of emergency sanctions on agricultural imports. In April as well both China and South Korea reacted angrily to approval of new Japanese textbooks that, in their view, whitewashed Japan's history of imperialism. South Korea recalled its ambassador as the halo from [South Korean leader] Kim Dae Jung's 1998 promise to leave history aside in bilateral relations began to fade. Then, in early May, the son of North Korea's leader was caught entering Japan illegally and hurriedly sent ahead to China without an investigation. That bizarre episode left a bitter aftertaste, especially among those on the Right who faulted the cabinet for not taking national sovereignty seriously. In May Tanaka and Koizumi also troubled relations with the United States by snubbing the new Bush administration when it called for a closer alliance and cooperation on National Missile Defense. Finally, Tanaka's May trip to Beijing caused consternation over an apparent tilt toward China. In the space of just weeks, therefore, Japan's relations with all its neighbors and most important partners seemed shorn of an anchor. But this tumble of events is not so surprising when looked at in the context of Japan's decade-long struggle for a larger international role and a new identity as an all-around great power seeking a requisite measure of global and regional influence.

A Bit Player

In the 1990s there was a great deal of talk about Japan's dual disappointments: dashed economic expectations and weak political leadership incapable of launching urgently needed domestic reforms. Missing from most of the discussions was mention of another grave disappointment: Japan's lack of clout in the international arena. After a half century of frustration as a defeated power obliged to lower its voice in the shadow of U.S. leadership in the Cold War and Asian memories of the Pacific War, Japan had failed to achieve its anticipated great power standing and regional leadership. Its flailing about in 2001 must be viewed against the backdrop of more than ten years of ill-conceived and unsuccessful foreign policy strategies.

Observers of Japanese national identity have paid inadequate attention to great power relations. One school of thought holds that Japan is similar to the United States in seeking to make its mark on the world through support for democracy, human rights, and a status quo balance of power. Thus it should welcome a stronger alliance with the United States aimed at closer coordination in dealings with China, Russia, and the Korean peninsula. The Bush administration took power in 2001 anticipating that Japan was inclined in this direction only to find a mixed response, more confused than negative. To be sure, European nations also objected to the Bush agenda, but Japan's caution was shaped by something more troublesome. A second school of thought emphasizes deep-seated ethnocentric attitudes associated with the concept of Nihonjinron—the logic of being Japanese. This thinking stresses the penchant of Japanese to see themselves as unique regardless of what international problem they are facing. (Chinese and Koreans often view Japanese foreign policy this way.) After the collapse of the bubble economy, the self-confidence behind this worldview was diminished, despite rising nationalism. While both approaches have merit, neither adequately explains Japan's foreign policy hopes and disappointments.

To do justice to the intense awareness of regional and great power competition in Japan, one must focus as well on elements of national identity manifested in strategies for gaining increased leverage, in global politics. These can be best observed in relations with five countries: the United States, China, Russia, South Korea, and North Korea. They are linked to Japanese efforts to translate economic power into other types of power, including political and cultural power, while reaching for more venues in which to display such power. Incorporating what Japanese say about their domestic strengths and weaknesses in global competition, this approach explores what we may call Japan's great power identity. . . .

Hopes for Leadership

In general, Japan in the 1980s experienced a decade of growing self-confidence in its economic power accompanied by a widening search for other types of power in Asia. At the start of the decade Prime Minister Masayoshi Ohira became known for his advocacy of Japanese cultural power: encouraging Japanese language study abroad, spreading the image of a superior model of management and social relations that fit well with Asian values, promoting traditional and popular Japanese culture as an alternative to U.S. cultural hegemony, and forging networks among business figures and politicians to allow regionalism to balance globalization. Japanese karaoke, animation, and even serial television dramas spread widely across East Asia over the decade, but still Japan lost ground to the United States as a cultural force. While Japan greatly expanded its economic ties to East and Southeast Asia after 1985 by transferring production abroad, such a vertical division of labor did not boost receptivity to its cultural exports, however impressive its bubble economy and trade surpluses.

As the 1990s began, China overtook the former Soviet Union as Japan's most significant other after the United States. Through the 1980s Japanese had, despite ups and downs, counted on China to respond. To a large degree, this was based on romanticism, as Japanese were overly optimistic about friendship with the Chinese people while viewing China more as part of East Asian civilization than as communist. Guilt among the older generation contributed to a tendency to give China the benefit of the doubt, even when setbacks to reform occurred. Moreover, Japanese observers were confident that China would remain weak and dependent on Japan's regional leadership. But what really fed Japanese anticipation was China's rift with the United States in the wake of Tiananmen Square. As a result, China became more open to regionalism and Japan offered itself as a champion of Asian values and a bridge between China's authoritarianism and the West's human rights agenda. With Japan's industrial juggernaut overtaking the United States in some high-tech industries and accumulating capital at an unprecedented rate, there was reason for optimism.

At the beginning of the 1990s Japanese were counting on three levers to boost their global stature. First, their prime ministers would shed the image of passivity in world affairs by speaking boldly at the G-7 [Group of Seven] summits and the United

Nations on the pressing issues of a new era: development assistance, environmental protection, and other nontraditional security matters. Second, their cash surplus would give them a voice of equal weight to that of the United States on international financial matters and a new say on military matters such as the Persian Gulf War. After all, America's appetite for leadership surpassed what its pocketbook could afford, creating a dependence on Japan. Third, the collapse of the socialist bloc left the world divided into three regional variants of capitalism, and Japan was the indisputable leader of the East Asian variant. With Asian dynamism continuing, Japanese saw their country leading the way into the twenty-first century. Great power expectations had dramatically grown from the reticent "economics alone" attitude prevalent through the 1970s. . . .

Offending Its Neighbors

The turning point came in 1995 when the Diet watered down a resolution of apology marking the fiftieth anniversary of the end of the Pacific War and many prefectural assemblies passed resolutions that rationalized the path of colonization and war that Japan had taken. History, it seemed, had come back to life to thwart Japan's aspirations again. The stage had been set in 1994 when Justice Minister Shigeto Nagano called the Nanking massacre of 1937 a "fabrication" and Shin Sakurai, director-general of the Environmental Agency, said that "Tokyo did not fight with the aim of waging a war of aggression, and Japan was not the only one that was wrong. Although we caused trouble to Asian nations, it was thanks to us that they were able to become independent." Such remarks by cabinet officials aroused all East Asia and elicited protests from Taipei as well as Beijing and Seoul. The rise in nationalism in both China and South Korea during the mid-1990s cannot be divorced from such provocations. Bolstered by lingering confidence in Japan's economic success combined with frustration over its foreign policy weakness, Japan's rightwing asserted a national identity both divisive in Asia and unsupportive of U.S. goals.

The four options Japanese had aspired to and believed were open to them in the early 1990s were thus closing down. First, the option of bankrolling Russia's transition to a market economy and opening to the economic dynamism of the Asia-Pacific region had faded. Russia's leaders preferred crony capitalism, corrupt profiteering, and massive capital flight to the model of China's open-door economy enticing international capital. Angered by Russia's refusal to negotiate the status of the islands in 1994–96, Japanese debated how they could punish Russia by withholding economic assistance even as the United States and Europe kept propping Yeltsin up with IMF loans, including funds drawn from Japan. Russo-Japanese relations declined, giving Japan little great power leverage and no relief to its claims of historical victimization.

Second, the steady advance of the Sino-Russian partnership relations from 1994 to 1996 closed off the Japanese strategy of guiding China's ascendance. Instead Beijing grew more assertive in its foreign policy, testing nuclear weapons after other countries had agreed to a moratorium, making a show of force to Taiwan when elections boosted the movement for independence, and joining Russia in denouncing (American) hegemony. Moreover, the Chinese Communist Party rode the fiftieth anniversary of the end of Japan's occupation to a new wave of nationalism to legitimate its historic role in overcoming national humiliation through repeated images of how evil Japan had been coupled with warnings of where it might be heading. Japanese public opinion had not anticipated this resurgent China. As China grew more confident, Japan could no longer expect to become a bridge between it and the United States. When the world awakened to China's soaring economy in 1993–96, as the World Bank recalculated its national product on the basis of purchasing power, double-digit growth became routine, and investment poured into the country. Japanese faced the prospect that their economy, now in prolonged stagnation, would not succeed in the vertical integration of East Asian regionalism. Public opinion lost hope in Japan as the regional leader just as it was turning sour on China as a friendly nation.

Third, relations with South Korea also worsened by 1996. Bolstered by their own new ties with China and Russia, cocky over their own bubble economy, and freed from authoritarian rule at last, the Koreans confidently explored the boundaries of their anger against Japan. When a flare-up over Tokdo (Takeshima) island occurred as both countries sought to define their 200-mile fishing zone, Koreans denounced Japan and Japanese were not shy about firing back, resenting rather than appeasing Korean nationalism.

Fourth, the Japanese awoke to the fact that the Clinton administration, despite an end to the divisive trade talks, was treating them with neglect. The Japanese in turn sensationalized a rape case in Okinawa as an example of the hazards of the American troop presence. To be sure, U.S. pressure had rescued Japan by stopping North Korea's nuclear weapons development program, but Japanese felt more burdened by the large costs they had been obliged to assume for the Korean Peninsula Development Organization (KEDO) project to supply an alternative energy source than grateful to the United States. There was little sentiment to return to the days of the Cold War, when Japan relied on the United States to take the initiative in foreign policy. But neither could Japan manage to place its alliance with Washington on a more equal footing.

Frustrated at Every Turn

In short, frustration gained the upper hand by the mid-1990s as Japanese felt thwarted in every direction. If politics had permitted, the timing might have been ideal for them to concentrate on a domestic agenda. The result could have been a revitalized Japan: with a streamlined bureaucracy to curtail "administrative guidance," a fiscal diet to reduce a mountain of deficits and pork-barrel spending, a decentralized polity to grant autonomy to local areas long stifled by Tokyo's red tape, and a school system that would promote creativity over rote memorization on entrance exams. But high-sounding goals never had a chance with politicians wedded to special interests. Unable to deliver much more than the semblance of reform, they looked instead to foreign affairs to boost their fading popularity. When the LDP secured power again, its leaders had a new determination to override the caution of the foreign affairs bureaucracy. . . .

Clinton's pursuit of China left the impression that after years of "Japan-bashing" during which the United States took Japan too seriously as a competitor, it was now engaged in "Japan passing" that did not take Japan seriously enough. So showcasing an artificial image of close Russian relations on the verge of a breakthrough, Tokyo's strategists made headway in limiting the damage. By strengthening defense ties to the United States and following the United States in rebuilding strained relations with China, Japan also managed to make its voice heard in triangular relations. If there was little cause for cheer, at least Japan was active in the parade of summits.

Then, in the second half of 1998, Japanese foreign relations turned topsy-turvy again. First, North Korea fired a missile over Japanese territory, causing a scare unlike anything in recent years. Japan appeared helpless against a growing military threat without any obvious place to find relief. Second, Kim Dae Jung agreed to an historic breakthrough in relations. In return for a written apology he pledged to drop the "historical card" and open South Korea to Japanese cultural products. This proved immensely popular in Japan, showing the way forward in a difficult region at a critical time. Third, Obuchi's summit with Yeltsin in Russia proved a bitter disappointment, although the blow was lessened by the restrained coverage in the Japanese media. Russia rejected Japan's offer of a "residual sovereignty" formula for the disputed islands, while Yeltsin's poor health cut short negotiations and made it appear that Japan was not taken seriously. Even worse, Jiang Zemin's November visit was a public relations disaster. Having postponed his trip until after the Kim Dae Jung visit due to floods in central China, Jiang could not wrest the same written apology the Koreans had gotten without a similar declaration about setting the past aside. Since he was unwilling to do that, the Japanese public railed against China's leaders for stirring up nationalism and aborting a future-oriented partnership. Japan had little to show for its great power maneuvering. . . .

Rising Patriotism

The events of the late 1990s bolstered the overall appeal of patriotism as the proper response to a dangerous world and a deteriorating domestic society. Shocks from China and North Korea and the decline of confidence in the United States all heightened insecurity. At the same time, fears about social disorder and alienation of youth compounded the impact of economic stagnation. The Diet's approval of the national anthem and rising-sun flag, which for a long time after the war had been relegated to unofficial use, signified a new determination about nationalism. The rightwing found a favorable environment to press its dual agenda: recapturing the moral high ground through vindicating Japanese history and winning a decisive victory in the court of public opinion over leftwing pacifism and defense of the postwar constitution: and forcing China, South Korea, and others to pay a high price for their nationalist criticisms of Japan. Bookstores showcased an unprecedented array of books trumpeting just how Japan should defend its national interests and pride. . . .

When Clinton left office without having had time to test North Korea's interest in a deal over its weapons programs, regional politics were left hanging. Given North Korea's reliance on military blackmail, there was no way to bypass U.S. leadership. At the start of 2001 Japan was pursuing Russia most avidly in the fear that the pursuit of North Korea by others would leave it isolated. Japan's hopes for China remained limited, but it was at least as nervous about the widening divide between the United States and China as it had been about Sino-U.S. deals. In short, Japanese had little confidence in their own diplomacy or that of others while Mori's approval ratings remained low and economic worries were spreading.

As the Bush administration made a shaky start in Asia, Japan independently brought about a deterioration in its relations with all of its Asian neighbors. First, a commission established to revise middle school history textbooks made recommendations that shocked the Chinese and Koreans and undid the progress made by the "apologies." Second, the mass media pounced on divisions within the Foreign Ministry over the new initiative to Putin to make the March 2001 Irkutsk summit (at which Putin recognized the validity of the 1956 treaty) appear to be a humiliating renunciation of Japanese insistence that all four islands be returned. Third, Japan acted to block a surge of Chinese agricultural imports, thereby provoking a trade war at the same time that it granted a visa to Taiwan's ex-president Lee Teng-hui. The Japanese public did not understand the logic that linked the various actions, but it was inclined to rally behind a defense of national sovereignty. When Koizumi took power in April and appointed Makiko Tanaka foreign minister, they symbolized a fresh start for a country under attack from all its neighbors and from the foreign policy professionals at home. They enjoyed extraordinary popularity as leaders prepared to act boldly. Koizumi tapped into rightwing support by insisting prior to July upper house elections that he would visit the Yasukuni shrine on August 15, the anniversary of Japan's surrender in World War II, to honor the war dead (later he compromised by moving the date of his visit to August 13). Tanaka reversed the policy toward Russia. Despite the absence of a clear strategy, they catered to nationalism. Tanaka's great popularity made Diet members think twice about questioning her closely even when she was seen as damaging the national interest through maverick behavior. . . .

The Nationalist Agenda

Voices on the right are now energized to pursue a nationalist agenda to challenge all obstacles at once. They insist that Mori's agenda with Putin be repudiated as Tokyo returns to the position of demanding all four islands in one batch while threatening economic retaliation if Moscow stalls. Likewise, the rightwing takes a tough line on China, urging deep cuts in Official Development Assistance (ODA), defiant support of Taiwan, and a military buildup if China does not limit its own armaments. To South Korea as well as China they deny any say about Japanese textbooks, insisting that it is strictly a matter for Japanese how they explain the causes and conduct of the decades of war and occupation. Finally, many on the right are ready to assert more independence from the United States, relying more on Japan's own armed forces. Facing severe economic problems and a difficult security environment, Tokyo does not have the luxury to pursue a nationalist agenda that could alienate many countries at once. Yet, leaders also dared not forgo the support of nationalism given the need to rally the Diet to defy powerful interest groups in making far-reaching reforms.

The mainstream in Japan recognizes that nationalism does not solve the country's principal problems. Japan needs regionalism as well as globalization. Given demographic and economic realities, its search for regional leadership will increasingly depend on its influence on the youth of Asia. Experts warn that at present Japan is losing the battle, notably for the rising Chinese intellectual elite who prefer American universities and companies. Japan needs an educational system that welcomes other Asians and eases the challenge of communicating with them. Such sober reasoning is eventually likely to prevail when regional tensions calm and domestic reforms advance. . . .

The upsurge in Japanese nationalism cannot bring any benefits in foreign relations despite temporary relief for feelings of weakness. It offers no prospects for regionalism in which Asians embrace Japan or great power balance in which pragmatism shapes policies. It leads to a national identity that drives Japan away from reform and globalization. Americans anxious about China may lend support to Japanese nationalism without realizing its long-term damage. Chinese anxious about the United States may some day do the same. Both of these countries should be prudent, recognizing Japan's need for a great power identity that will maintain an independent posture and a mix of civilizational associations but fearing the consequences of rekindled nationalism. It will take a rise in confidence in Japan's domestic prospects and its great power stature to support a future-oriented national identity. In the coming age of globalization, Japan will likely combine three identities. First, new reforms aimed at economic efficiency will reinforce a shared global identity widely associated with Western civilization but not limited to it. Having associated their fate with that of the West in the Cold War era, Japanese have a good foundation for a global identity. Second, rising nationalism, as seen in the 1990s, brings to the surface a distinctive Japanese civilization, whose symbols are likely to be further reinforced in an age of confused identities. Prudent politicians need to manage this nationalism without exacerbating it. Finally, the revival of regionalism is bound to raise the profile of a shared Confucian tradition as an alternative to aspects of Western civilization. Such a vision could prompt cooperation with China and the Koreas and need not be a threat to the United States. A mélange of identities may leave foreign policy vacillating, but it offers the best way forward in difficult times.

Insecurity and Hope in the New Era

By Masaru Tamamoto

Following the so-called "lost decade" of the 1990s, many Japanese struggled to understand what had gone wrong. It was not just that Japan's economy failed to restart after the collapse of speculative investments in 1990. Many Japanese felt their nation had come adrift and lost its sense of purpose, unity, and social order. Yet not every change was for the worse. Japanese women, long trapped in strictly defined roles, began to wrest unprecedented freedom from their society. Even some men broke out of the postwar "salaryman" mold and explored new and liberating lifestyles. Economic insecurity, however, gnawed at the national psyche. The anxiety was made worse by the apparent inability of elected officials to remedy the situation. In the following essay, written in fall 2000, Masaru Tamamoto, a Japanese intellectual, takes a stark look at his society and its prospects.

An unhappy listlessness best describes the gloom that continues to grip Japan after a decade of recession, the longest bout of economic [2000] downturn since 1945. This was evident at the polls this summer when the floundering Liberal Democrats and their unpopular prime minister, Yoshiro Mori, were narrowly reelected almost by default, since the opposition seemed even more ineffectual.

The gloom is evident in the press, as in a typical article in the influential national daily, *Asahi*, quoting a stock market insider as predicting that the once-powerful yen will in ten years lose half its value. And it is apparent in classrooms, the workplace, and the home, where decisions about jobs and marriage are rooted in an

Masaru Tamamoto, "Japan and Its Discontents: A Letter from Yokohama," *World Policy Journal*, vol. 17, Fall 2000, pp. 41–49. Copyright © 2000 by *World Policy Journal*. Reproduced by permission.

abiding pessimism about the future. Yet ironically, the national traits that were once seen as the secret of Japan's economic success—stability, consensus, and homogeneity—appear to contribute powerfully to the sense of drift. This has to be a matter of prudent concern to America, Japan's principal trading partner. The question is, what went wrong?

Ineffective Borrowing

The last time Japan faced economic hardship was in the 1970s. During the oil crises of 1973 and 1979, the country, almost wholly dependent on imported energy, panicked. But we knew what had to be done. We rushed to build nuclear power plants. We diversified foreign sources of oil and gas; in the process, Indonesia became the recipient of massive Japanese foreign aid in exchange for the promise of a stable supply of energy. That was the beginning of Japan's heavy involvement with the economies of Southeast Asia. We cultivated more independent diplomatic relations with the Arab countries and Iran, becoming less dependent on American leadership and freer to make our own deals. We worked harder and longer, improving efficiency and raising productivity. A cruel consequence of this effort was an increase in the number of deaths from overwork, but even that seemed to be part of what was necessary. As a result, Japan achieved the highest growth rate among the G-7 economies save Canada, an energy-rich country with a small population.

The story today [2000] is altogether different. We are ten years into a recession and nothing effective has been done to remedy the slump. Worse, we are reminded almost daily by the government that we are in for a hard time, for a long time. If the government is to be believed, we have already mortgaged the standard of living of our children and grandchildren.

The government has been spending massively on public construction projects and bailing out banks in recent years, which has barely kept the economy afloat. This spending has been backed by borrowing through issuing bonds. As a result, Japan is by far the most indebted of the G-7 economies and carries the biggest debt as a percentage of GDP (about 250 percent) ever owed by any developed country in peacetime. While the theoretical limit to government borrowing is hard to ascertain—and the bulk of the bond purchases are made by Japanese rather than by foreigners, which makes bonds less likely to be dumped in a panic—

the government cannot continue much longer to borrow and spend at the present rate in order to prop up the economy. The world has turned topsy turvy since 1990, the year Japan's bubble burst, when the Japanese government was running a bigger budget surplus than the United States enjoys today.

An Aging Nation

There is a hint of good news amid the gloom. Business investment, though limited to large firms in the high-tech sector, began to pick up this spring. Investment had been curtailed as a result of excess capacity caused by overinvestment during 1985–90, the bubble years, and during the early phase of the recession, when the cost of capital was cheap. Corporations reduced their investment, waiting for consumer demand to pick up. Now, however, corporate Japan is awakening to the need to invest in information technology. (Up to this point, Japan has stood on the sidelines of the "new economy" as the United States zoomed past.) We can only hope that this may lead to sustained economic growth, while casting a wary eye on the American "bubble," whose collapse, when it comes, will surely drag the Japanese economy down. (Our own experience makes us uneasy observers of the present American exuberance—we were once there.)

Still, we are warned by our government that the economic upturn, when it comes, will not solve the debt problem, because Japan is aging rapidly, faster than any G-7 society except Italy. In the year 2020, one in four Japanese will be over 65 years old. Fewer productive people will support an increasing number of the old and sick. Social security and national medical insurance schemes, designed on the assumption that the era of high economic growth would continue indefinitely, are already verging on insolvency. As things stand, young people will see only a fraction of their social security contributions when the time comes for them to retire; thus many refuse to participate. The costs of caring for the old and sick, which the indebted government cannot afford, will certainly continue to rise.

New laws are being enacted to shift the financial burden of caring for the elderly back to the people. We also know that the government is anxiously waiting for the economy to recover so taxes can be raised to begin to cover the deficit. For the government, relatively speaking, there is room to maneuver—Japan's tax revenue as a percentage of GDP is the lowest among the G-7 countries. Thus the prospect of an economic upturn is dampened by the realization of the higher taxes that will accompany it.

Small wonder, then, that Japanese consume less and save more than before the onslaught of the recession. Moreover, the current unemployment rate adds to the problem of low consumption. At slightly less than 5 percent, unemployment is the highest it has been since the turmoil of the immediate postwar era. This figure seems low by American and European standards, but in the Japanese system of lifetime employment, it is alarmingly high. And there is still redundancy in employment, which if eliminated could raise the jobless rate to 8 percent. In a recent poll, nearly 70 percent of respondents feared losing their jobs. So the boost in consumption necessary to bring the economy out of its current doldrums cannot be counted on. The future seems too bleak for people to spend, but their curtailed spending only makes the future bleaker.

A notable difference between the Japan of the oil crises and the Japan of the current recession is the loss of a sense of unity and shared fate. During the earlier crisis, people worked together toward economic recovery. Many corporate employees were reassigned to subsidiaries and accepted a reduction in pay, while corporations generally honored the practice of lifetime employment. That was "Japan, Inc." Now the sense of unity has all but evaporated. Corporations, to remain solvent and regain competitiveness, have begun to dismiss employees. The mainstay of the Japanese system, lifetime employment and seniority, is crumbling. By the end of the 1990s, most corporations had already announced their adherence to this fundamental shift in employment policy: By 1997, only a third sought to retain the policy of lifetime employment. In the following year, the figure was down to 26 percent, and by 1999, only 6 percent of corporations still planned to maintain the old system. "Japan, Inc." was out of business.

This transformation can be understood as a rational economic move, approximating normal capitalistic behavior by putting the interest of stockholders above that of employees and seeking profit over market share. But socially, the end of lifetime employment and seniority fundamentally alters the post-1945 Japanese social contract to the point of betrayal. Two age groups are particularly affected—university students and middle-aged corporate employees.

Corporations have been keen to fire the middle-aged, many of whom had risen to middle-level positions in a predictable fashion under the seniority system. As pay increased proportionately with tenure, those who found themselves suddenly out of work were just about to reap the benefits of three decades of labor. Their life plans—and how else could they have planned?—rested on the stability of the system. How now to make the mortgage payment?

Compared to America's relatively fluid labor market, Japan's is inflexible. Unemployed older workers in particular find new jobs extremely hard to come by. Personal bankruptcies have risen by a factor of eight in the last ten years, with much of the increase coincident with the beginning of corporate layoffs. Coincident also is the number of suicides—a 30 percent increase between 1997 and 1998. Men in their forties and fifties accounted for a third of all suicides and for much of the increase. Most of them were the recently unemployed, who chose a life insurance payment as the final legacy to their families. Life insurance companies, rationally reflecting the mores of a new era, are now reconsidering their policy of paying out for death by suicide.

For their part, the sons of the middle-aged—now jobless or fearing dismissal—constitute a generation that feels betrayed. The evidence is their fathers' predicament. The impact of the recession on the young is certain to determine the direction and future shape of Japan. It is not simply that university graduates are finding fewer jobs. Rather, it is the erosion of the well-understood rules that, until recently, guided mainstream Japanese life. The hurdles under the old formula were a series of examinations, starting in kindergarten and continuing through grade school, middle school, high school, university, and finally the corporation. These examinations were standardized, with model answers, and students sought to memorize the answers by rote. After-school cram schools, running late into the evening, were part of the formula. All this greatly cramped childhood. Today's university students made the necessary sacrifices, only to find that the rules of the game have suddenly changed.

Corporate recruiters used to ask from which university a person had graduated. Now they ask: What skills do you have that the company needs? How are you different from and better than the other applicants? Too many graduates simply do not know how to respond. University life once offered a moment of reprieve between examination hell and the daily grind of corporate life. Except for those who choose a technical education, the majority in liberal arts acquire few skills beyond those gleaned in high school. A change in the purpose and content of a university education, which would involve the entire education system, has become a major national controversy as a result of the rewriting of the social contract spurred by the recession.

The Post-Developmental Era

But why are seemingly sensible new questions by corporate recruiters so out of place in Japan? The answer lies in the structure of the so-called developmental state that arose from the ashes of the Second World War.

Although Japan's economy was shattered at war's end, it nonetheless possessed tremendous potential for growth and development. Before surrender, Japan had, after all, possessed enough power to command an empire and wage a prolonged war in Asia against China, the United States, and Britain. And while defeat stripped Japan of empire, and with it the control of natural resources, the average Japanese worker could be trained for jobs requiring a high level of skill. Thus the strategy of the postwar developmental state was to import technology and to invest aggressively in human capital.

In the early postwar years, high schools and universities did not produce enough graduates who could be of immediate use to business. So corporations took on the task of long-term training and investment in human capital. In order not to lose workers after investing so much in them, corporations set up a system in which the benefit to the worker increased the longer he stayed within a system of lifetime employment and seniority.

Under this system, corporations were unable to shed workers in times of downturn. To obviate the risk, corporate Japan established the so-called keiretsu system of long-term contracts and stable cross-holding of shares. The government, in turn, curbed what it deemed "excessive" competition by raising regulatory barriers to new entrants. At the same time, it created an incentive structure for workers to stay within the company. The government provided sparse health insurance and pension benefits to the population in general while giving tax incentives to corporations to offer added benefits to the long-term worker.

The developmental state produced remarkable results. (One wonders, though, whether a more efficient laissez-faire approach would have created a higher growth pattern, albeit with greater social disharmony.) Workers gained security at the expense of certain freedoms. They could not change jobs easily since the rigid seniority structure made movement difficult. Until recently, no bank, for example, would hire a former worker of any other bank, no matter how talented that worker, for fear of upsetting the system. Furthermore, workers could not move their pension schemes to new places of employment.

The developmental state now suffers from structural fatigue. There is growing recognition that future prosperity depends upon fundamental change. The myriad regulations to ensure stability and order are too rigid for the new age of information technology and globalizing capitalism. As we have seen, corporations have already introduced layoffs as an acceptable practice, and they are beginning to disentangle themselves from the keiretsu web, seeking profit over stability. They even raid rivals for talent. In response, the government is considering instituting an American-type 401(k) retirement plan to encourage mobility of labor. The worker thus is set free, and made to feel insecure.

Corporate restructuring is essential if Japan is to recover from the recession. With successful restructuring, perhaps in two or three years the Japanese economy may manage a respectable, sustained growth rate of 2 percent or so. Yet this is not unalloyed good news for ordinary people, since successful restructuring will mean a prolonged level of high unemployment.

New Roles for Women

The developmental state created a gendered division of labor. The woman's place of work was at home, raising children and caring for the ill and elderly. Women were expected to provide social services that otherwise the government would have had to furnish. Both corporate and government policies provided little inducement for women to act as workers outside the home for the long term. Corporations offered women unequal pay and expected them to resign upon marriage. The government structured health and pension schemes so that a woman benefited from them as a dependent of her husband. This scheme of things is also beginning to break down.

As things stand, daycare for children is woefully inadequate. And how will the elderly be cared for? In terms of meeting the pending labor shortage, the recruitment of women is a double-edged sword. Japanese society is aging not only because people are living longer but because women are having fewer babies. At the present fertility rate, Japan's population will begin to decline in seven years, and as more women pursue careers outside the home, the rate of decline of births is likely to increase. The behavior of young women has also changed during the recession of the past decade. The proportion of women in their late twenties who are married has declined in a decade from one-half to one-third, and the link between marriage and having children has weakened. Increasingly, married women are choosing to have no children, or to bear fewer children later, and remain in the work force. This has an economic logic. On average, a child consumes 17 percent of household income, two children 25 percent. And a woman who stops working can forfeit a half million dollars in lost wages and reduced pension. There is also a certain honesty in a young woman's choice to have no, or fewer, children since it breaks the traditional expectation of the parent to be taken care of in old age by the child. Women today increasingly refuse to care for aging parents as the social structure changes.

Another consequence of these various societal changes is less tolerance of violence. Japan is not known to be a violent place. Society is orderly and peaceful, as the low crime rate attests. But this pertains to physical violence. There is much psychological violence in everyday life in terms of the humiliation and embarrassment that arise from an authoritarian social structure. Rank and knowing one's place are key supports of the well-known Japanese attributes of consensus and conformity. In such a rigidly hierarchical society, the humiliated and embarrassed are unable to fight back to preserve their self-esteem. The opportunity for assertion comes from the twisted ability to humiliate and embarrass those below. The high level of alcohol consumption is not unrelated to this omnipresent psychological violence.

Japanese have tolerated this kind of violence because of the benefit of conformity—a predictable and secure life. But now the benefit is dissipating. With the demise of corporate lifetime employment, the whole system of seniority in Japanese life—of hierarchy and authoritarian manners and rigid ranking—is losing its coherence. As the promise of a predictable and secure life is withdrawn, tolerance of psychological violence decreases.

Seeking Stability

The reaction of the young to the changing situation is mixed. In a recent opinion poll, seven out of ten high school graduates said they wished to be employed by the government. They were not, on the whole, motivated by devotion to public service but by the expectation that the practice of lifetime employment and seniority would continue in government jobs. On the other hand, even before the wave of corporate layoffs in recent years, one in three high school and university graduates had quit their jobs in the first three years of employment. Many among the young are conversely searching for values other than predictability and security. Societal values are diversifying and the privilege of choosing is becoming a noticeable facet of Japanese life. Still, the choices are not straightforward. Although many young women continue to say that they prefer to marry and stay at home, the lure of money leads them to remain single and continue to work.

The recession has shown that the old set of preferences can no longer be met. Security and safety, and "sameness" and equality of result were previously society's main values and goals. Japanese life is becoming less secure and more unequal. The end of lifetime employment and seniority means greater income differences among employees. Corporations, which hitherto operated in a heavily regulated environment, are now vying for skilled managers. The making of a more competitive and harsher society is inevitable. But government—politicians and bureaucrats alike—has been slow to accept the inevitable, to make the hard choices. As a result, Japan continues to flounder. . . .

The Japanese government may be slow in adjusting to the new economy, but it cannot buck the trend. The president of Sony, a manufacturing company of electronics goods now rapidly remaking itself in order to participate in the new economy, likens information and technology to a meteor smashing through the crust of old Japanese ways.

While pessimism rules in Japan today, it would be silly to underestimate Japan's potential for resurgence. Though much has to change, especially in the sphere of government, not everything has to change in an economy that has worked well for half a century. Whether the Japanese people will be happier in a society freer, more competitive, and unequal, in a society more like the United States, is another question.

Chronology

ca. 30,000–10,000 B.C.
Hunter-gatherers migrate across land bridges from Asia into Japan.

7000 B.C.
Earliest Jōmon pottery begins to appear in archaeological record, along with large mounds of shellfish, indicating a hunter-gatherer lifestyle.

300 B.C.
The Jōmon period comes to an end as a fresh wave of migration from Korea results in the Yayoi civilization taking hold in Japan. With it, rice farming emerges.

A.D. 300
The Yamato, successors to the Yayoi, unite the nation and build giant earth-mound tombs known as *kofun*. Chinese records suggest that at this time Japan is ruled by female monarchs.

538
Buddhism and writing enter Japan from China.

604
Prince Shotoku proclaims a seventeen-article constitution for Japan.

710
The Fujiwara clan takes control, and Nara becomes the first official capital of Japan.

712
The *Kojiki*, Japan's oldest surviving document, is compiled at the imperial court.

794
Japan's capital moves to Kyoto (then known as Heian-kyo).

ca. 1005
Lady Murasaki begins writing the world's first novel, *The Tale of Genji*, based on her experiences at the imperial court.

1159
Taira Kiyomori gains control over Japan following his clan's victory in feudal wars.

1191
New sects of Japanese Buddhism, such as Zen, flourish.

1192
Yoritomo, the first of Japan's shoguns, sets up a "tent government" at Kamakura, as his Minamoto clan seizes power from the Taira clan.

1274
The Mongols attempt an invasion of Japan and are repelled, in part by bad weather.

1281
The Mongols attempt a second invasion. Storms again destroy much of their fleet, giving rise to the myth of a kamikaze ("divine wind") protecting Japan. (Nearly seven centuries later, that myth will inspire a suicidal defense of the homeland against American armed forces at the end of World War II.)

1333
The Kamakura government crumbles.

1334
Emperor Godaigo briefly restores the imperial house to power.

1336
The Ashikaga clan forces Godaigo to abdicate; warlord rule is reestablished but faces frequent and bloody challenges.

1467
The ten-year-long Onin civil war, one of Japan's bloodiest, erupts.

1542
European sailors arrive, introducing firearms, Christianity, and bread to Japan.

1549

Francis Xavier founds the first Christian mission in Japan at Kagoshima.

1573

Oda Nobunaga, a ruthless and determined general, gains victory over the last of his rivals. He patronizes Christianity, increasing its spread.

1582

Oda is assassinated before he can complete his consolidation of national power. Taiko Hideyoshi, a peasant turned general in Oda's army, becomes shogun and completes the task.

1587

Under Hideyoshi's patronage, the great tea master Sen-no-Rikyu establishes the tea ceremony as a highly important Japanese ritual.

1598

Hideyoshi dies.

1600

Tokugawa Ieyasu, a general under Hideyoshi, displaces his former leader's son and goes on to defeat the last of his rivals in the Battle of Sekigahara.

1603

Ieyasu becomes the first of the Tokugawa shoguns and shifts the capital to Edo, now known as Tokyo.

1614

A ban on Christianity is extended nationwide.

1639

Edicts establishing national isolation are completed. The Japanese are forbidden to travel abroad, and all Westerners except the Dutch are prohibited from entering Japan.

1688

The Genroku era, a period of flourishing Japanese arts such as Kabuki theater and Bunraku puppetry, begins. It will last until 1704.

1853

Commodore Matthew Perry leads a U.S. fleet across the Pacific to deliver a demand that Japan open its ports to trade.

1854

Under the threat of warships in its harbors, Japan signs the Treaty of Peace and Amity with the United States.

1858

The Harris Treaty establishes U.S. trading rights in Japan. Other Western powers soon follow, imposing a series of "unequal treaties" upon Japan.

1867–1868

The last shogun resigns and the Meiji Restoration occurs. Emperor Mutsuhito (posthumously known as Meiji) takes power.

1889

The Meiji Constitution is proclaimed, establishing a parliament under the sovereignty of the emperor.

1890

The Imperial Rescript on Education sets the goals of education and family in terms of service to the state.

1894–1895

Japan goes to war against China over which nation will dominate Korea. Japan's crushing victory marks its emergence as a world power.

1904–1905

Japan defeats Russia in a war that culminates in a naval battle in the Straits of Tsushima.

1910

Japan annexes Korea, beginning thirty-five years of colonial rule.

1911

Women's rights advocate Hiratsuka Raicho founds the magazine *Seito* (*Bluestocking*), which becomes a centerpiece for Japanese women's creative and aesthetic endeavors.

1912

Emperor Meiji dies; his son, Taisho, succeeds him.

1914
Japan enters World War I on the side of the Allies.

1920–1921
Japan gains limited great-power recognition in the League of Nations and the postwar treaty system. Parliamentary rule makes its first real strides in Japan, leading to what historians will later call the Taisho Democracy period.

1921
Crown Prince Hirohito is named regent as a result of his father's mental instability.

1923
The Great Kanto Earthquake destroys much of Tokyo and surrounding areas; Korean residents are massacred in the riots that follow.

1926
Hirohito, already regent, becomes emperor following the death of Emperor Taisho. (Hirohito is now known as Emperor Showa.)

1931
Japan's imperial army stages the "Manchurian Railway Incident," which leads to the creation of the Japanese-controlled state of Manchukuo within China.

1937
A second war with China erupts; Japan's victorious imperial army rampages against civilians in the Chinese capital of Nanjing.

1941
Japan launches a surprise attack against the U.S. fleet at Pearl Harbor; World War II expands into the Pacific.

1945
Japan surrenders unconditionally on September 2, after suffering devastating atom-bomb attacks on Hiroshima and Nagasaki. The Allied Occupation, led by U.S. general Douglas MacArthur, begins.

1946

A constitution drafted by MacArthur's staff is adopted by Japan's Diet; Emperor Showa renounces his divinity and becomes "symbol of the people."

1952

The Treaty of San Francisco officially brings occupation to an end. Japan and the Soviet Union remain in dispute over ownership of Soviet-occupied islands north of Hokkaido.

1956

Japan, its economy rapidly recovering thanks to contracts to supply U.S. forces battling in Korea, becomes a member of the United Nations.

1964

Tokyo hosts the summer Olympic Games and makes the most of an opportunity to showcase Japan's postwar economic progress.

1972

Japan, following the U.S.'s lead, establishes normal diplomatic relations with Communist-ruled China.

1973

The first "oil shock" (resulting from the Organization of Petroleum Exporting Countries' boycott in support of the Arab war against Israel) staggers Japan's oil-dependent economy.

1984

Recovering from a recession, Japan's economy begins a boom that will briefly make the Tokyo stock market the richest in the world.

1989

Emperor Showa dies after a long battle with cancer; his son Akihito becomes emperor of the Heisei era.

1990

Japan's stock bubble bursts and its real estate prices begin to plummet.

1993

Beset by scandal and an inability to solve the country's economic crisis, the Liberal Democratic Party loses its parliamentary majority in the Diet for the first time since 1947, leading to a short-lived coalition government formed by liberal reformers and socialists.

1995

The Hanshin earthquake levels much of the port city of Kobe, leaving more than six thousand people dead and hundreds of thousands homeless; Aum Shinrikyo, a radical Japanese Buddhist cult, releases deadly sarin gas in a terrorist attack on Tokyo's subways; a dozen people lose their lives, and more than five thousand are injured.

1996

The Liberal Democratic Party regains its majority in the Diet.

2001

After years of worry regarding the continuation of the imperial line, an heir is born to Crown Prince Naruhito and Princess Masako. However, the baby is a girl, and Japanese law limits the imperial line to males.

FOR FURTHER RESEARCH

Historical Overviews

W.G. Beasley, *The Japanese Experience: A Short History of Japan.* Berkeley and Los Angeles: University of California Press, 1999.

Noel F. Busch, *The Horizon Concise History of Japan.* New York: American Heritage, 1972.

John Whitney Hall, *Japan: From Prehistory to Modern Times.* New York: Delacorte Press, 1970.

John Whitney Hall et al., eds., *The Cambridge History of Japan.* New York: Cambridge University Press, 1988.

Kenneth G. Henshall, *A History of Japan: From Stone Age to Superpower.* New York: St. Martin's Press, 1999.

David J. Lu, *Japan: A Documentary History.* Armonk, NY: M.E. Sharpe, 1997.

Milton W. Meyer, *Japan: A Concise History.* 3rd ed. Savage, MD: Rowman & Littlefield, 1993.

W. Scott Morton, *Japan: Its History and Culture.* New York: McGraw-Hill, 1994.

Louis G. Perez, *The History of Japan.* Westport, CT: Greenwood Press, 1998.

Edwin O. Reischauer, *Japan: The Story of a Nation.* New York: McGraw-Hill, 1989.

Conrad Totman, *A History of Japan.* Malden, MA: Blackwell, 2000.

Ancient History

J. Edward Kidder Jr., *Japan Before Buddhism.* New York: Praeger, 1966.

Feudal Era

Robert N. Bellah, *Tokugawa Religion: The Cultural Roots of Modern Japan.* New York: Free Press, 1985.

Harold Bolitho, *Treasures Among Men: The Fudai Daimyo in Tokugawa Japan.* New Haven, Yale University Press, 1974.

Susan B. Hanley, *Everyday Things in Premodern Japan: The Hidden Legacy of Material Culture.* Berkeley and Los Angeles: University of California Press, 1997.

Marius Jansen, ed., *Warrior Rule in Japan.* New York: Cambridge University Press, 1995.

Transition to Modernism

Pat Barr, *The Coming of the Barbarians: The Opening of Japan to the West 1853–1870.* New York: E.P. Dutton, 1967.

Marius B. Jansen and Gilbert Rozman, eds., *Japan in Transition, from Tokugawa to Meiji.* Princeton, NJ: Princeton University Press, 1986.

Donald Keene, *Emperor of Japan: Meiji and His World, 1852–1912.* New York: Columbia University Press, 2002.

Modern History

W.G. Beasley, *Japanese Imperialism 1894–1945.* Oxford, England: Oxford University Press, 1987.

———, *The Rise of Modern Japan.* 2nd ed. New York: St. Martin's Press, 1995.

Andrew Gordon, *The Modern History of Japan: From Tokugawa Times to the Present.* New York: Oxford University Press, 2003.

Mikiso Hane, *Modern Japan: A Historical Survey.* Boulder, CO: Westview Press, 1986.

James L. Huffman, *Modern Japan: An Encyclopedia of History, Culture, and Nationalism.* New York: Garland, 1998.

Janet E. Hunter, *The Emergence of Modern Japan: An Introductory History Since 1853.* London and New York: Longman, 1989.

Marius B. Jansen, *The Making of Modern Japan*. Cambridge, MA: Belknap Press of Harvard University Press, 2000.

James L. McClain, *Japan: A Modern History*. New York: W.W. Norton, 2002.

Tessa Morris-Suzuki, *Showa: An Inside History of Hirohito's Japan*. London: Athlone Press, 1984.

Takafusa Nakamura, *A History of Showa Japan, 1926–1989*. Tokyo: University of Tokyo Press, 1998.

J.E. Thomas, *Modern Japan: A Social History Since 1868*. London and New York: Longman, 1996.

Modern Japan at War

Stephen Howarth, *The Fighting Ships of the Rising Sun: The Drama of the Imperial Japanese Navy, 1895–1945*. New York: Atheneum, 1983.

Edwin P. Hoyt, *The Kamikazes: Suicide Squadrons of World War II*. Springfield, NJ: Burford Books, 1999.

Yuki Tanaka, with Toshiyuki Tanaka, *Japan's Comfort Women: The Military and Involuntary Prostitution During War and Occupation*. London: Routledge, 2001.

Nicholas Tarling, *A Sudden Rampage: The Japanese Occupation of Southeast Asia, 1941–1945*. Honolulu: University of Hawaii Press, 2001.

Atomic Bombings

Frank Barnaby and Douglas Holdstock, eds., *Hiroshima and Nagasaki: Retrospect and Prospect*. Portland, OR: F. Cass, 1995.

John W. Dower, "Hiroshima, Nagasaki, and the Politics of Memory," *Technology Review*, August/September 1995.

John Hersey, *Hiroshima*. New York: Knopf, 1946.

Richard H. Minear, trans. and ed., *Hiroshima: Three Witnesses*. Princeton, NJ: Princeton University Press, 1990.

U.S.-Led Occupation of Japan

Roger Buckley, *Occupation Diplomacy: Britain, the United States, and Japan, 1945–1952*. New York: Cambridge University Press, 1982.

Theodore Cohen, *Remaking Japan: The American Occupation as New Deal*. New York: Free Press, 1987.

Richard B. Finn, *Winners in Peace: MacArthur, Yoshida, and Postwar Japan*. Berkeley and Los Angeles: University of California Press, 1992.

U.S. Naval Historical Center, "Japan Capitulates, August–September 1945." www.history.navy.mil.

R.E. Ward and Y. Sakamoto, *Democratizing Japan: The Allied Occupation*. Honolulu: University of Hawaii Press, 1987.

Postwar History

Roger Buckley, *Japan Today*. Cambridge, England: Cambridge University Press, 1998.

John W. Dower, *Embracing Defeat: Japan in the Wake of World War II*. New York: W.W. Norton, 1999.

George Fields, *From Bonsai to Levi's*. New York: Macmillan, 1985.

Ezra Vogel, *Japan's New Middle Class*. Berkeley and Los Angeles: University of California Press, 1963.

Contemporary Issues

Norma Field, *In the Realm of a Dying Emperor: A Portrait of Japan at Century's End*. New York: Knopf, 1993.

Martin Muhleisen and Hamid Faruqee, "Japan Population Aging and the Fiscal Challenge," *Finance & Development*, March 2001.

Clayton Naff, *About Face: How I Stumbled onto Japan's Social Revolution*. New York: Kodansha International, 1994. Rev. paperback edition, 1996.

National Defense Counsel for Victims of Karoshi, *Karoshi ["Death by Overwork"]: When the "Corporate Warrior" Dies*. Tokyo: Mado-Sha, 1990.

Jonathan Rauch, *The Outnation: A Search for the Soul of Japan*. Boston: Little, Brown, 1992.

Cultural History

Michiko Yamaguchi Aoki, *Ancient Myths and Early History of Japan: A Cultural Foundation*. New York: Exposition Press, 1974.

Ruth Benedict, *The Chrysanthemum and the Sword: Patterns of Japanese Culture*. Boston: Houghton Mifflin, 1946.

Samuel L. Leiter, ed., *A Kabuki Reader: History and Performance*. Armonk, NY: M.E. Sharpe, 2001.

Kakzuo Okakura, *The Book of Tea*. New York: Dover, 1964.

G.B. Sansom, *Japan: A Short Cultural History*. Rev. ed. Stanford, CA: Stanford University Press, 1953.

Kisshomaru Ueshiba, *The Spirit of Aikido*. Tokyo: Kodansha International, 1987.

Fukuzawa Yukichi, *The Autobiography of Fukuzawa Yukichi*. New York: Columbia University Press, 1966.

Memoirs and Eyewitness Accounts

Hugh Cortazzi, ed., *Mitford's Japan: The Memoirs and Recollections, 1866–1906, of Algernon Bertram Mitford, the First Lord Redesdale*. London: Athlone Press, 1985.

Mark Gayn, *Japan Diary*. New York: W. Sloane Associates, 1948.

John Junkerman, ed., *Dear General MacArthur: Letters from the Japanese During the American Occupation*. Trans. Shizue Matsuda. Lanham, MD: Rowman & Littlefield, 2001.

Kenzaburo Oe, *Japan, the Ambiguous, and Myself: The Nobel Prize Speech and Other Lectures*. Tokyo: Kodansha International, 1995.

Elizabeth Gray Vining, *Windows for the Crown Prince*. Philadelphia: Lippincott, 1952.

Women's History

Gail Lee Bernstein, ed., *Recreating Japanese Women, 1600–1945*. Berkeley and Los Angeles: University of California Press, 1991.

Marjorie Wall Bingham and Susan Hill Gross, *Women in Japan: From Ancient Times to the Present*. St. Louis Park, MN: Glenhurst, 1987.

INDEX